UNDERSTAND
YOUR
ACCOUNTS

UNDERSTAND YOUR ACCOUNTS

Second Edition

A St J Price

**Kogan
Page**

First published in 1978 by Lynxplan (Sheffield) Ltd
Revised edition published in 1979 and reprinted 1981;
second edition 1986, reprinted 1986; both published by
Kogan Page Ltd
120 Pentonville Road, London N1 9JN

British Library Cataloguing in Publication Data

Price, A. St. J.
    Understand your accounts. — 2nd ed.
    1. Corporations — Accounting 2. Financial
    statements
    I. Title
    657'.95   HF5686.C7

    ISBN 0 85038 968 2 Pbk

Printed and bound in Great Britain by
Biddles Ltd, Guildford and King's Lynn

Contents

Introduction

The first edition of *Understand Your Accounts* was reprinted verbatim from the second edition of a larger book, *Profit from Figures, Financial Control for Non Accountants*.

However, some people are a little daunted by the scope of *Profit from Figures*. Accounts are so much of a mystery that they prefer to take one step at a time, to grasp the meaning of their annual accounts before tackling budgets.

Understand Your Accounts shows you how to read a balance sheet. It strips the mystery away from figures and helps you to ask more sensible questions about them, which gives you better value from your accountants.

This second edition of *Understand Your Accounts* includes much new material and many minor revisions. Already proven in practice, I am sure that it will give you the confidence to cope with numbers.

How to use this book

If you find difficulty with any point, leave it and carry on. Read the whole book through quickly and then revise it more slowly. This is the easiest way to master any problems. Each section contains questions or exercises to check your understanding.

A St J Price, FCA
Circencester
June 1985

Part 1
What It's All About

Chapter 1

Why You Need Financial Controls in Your Business

Business is a high risk activity: long-term success does not usually come easily. Many people fail because it is tough, not because they deserve to lose. Enthusiasm, hard work, intelligence — these attributes do not guarantee survival. Only generating cash will do that. Financial control adequate to ensure that there's cash to pay the bills is usually the ingredient whose absence leads to business failure.

You don't *have* to have good financial control to win in business — but without it your chances are much lower. In fact you are gambling, not managing.

So financial control is about maximising your chances of survival and making sure that no one disaster can sink you. It enables you to grab the opportunities and maximise your good luck while avoiding some of the bad luck and minimising the rest.

Why financial control will maximise your chances of survival

You can't run a business without money. Whatever other reasons you may have for being in business, making money is vital. Without it your business will fail.

To survive in the short term you have to be able to pay the bills. That means making sure that your activities result in enough cash in the bank to meet your liabilities as they become due. It takes a good grip on the financial aspects of a business to make sure the money is available when needed.

To succeed in the long term, you must make a profit as well. While it's cash that pays the bills, it's profits which will keep you in business. Over the longer term, you must make sufficient profit to be able to finance the growth of the business and to invest in the equipment, premises or whatever is needed to ensure its future prosperity.

Profit and cash are not the same. It's all too common for a business to make a profit without enough cash coming in to keep it going. Profit tends to get tied up in stocks, debtors, equipment etc. If this results in a shortage of cash to pay the bills, you cannot trade properly but must waste time and energy fending off your creditors. Once such crises begin, they tend to become worse and worse until, eventually, you may have to close down or sell out. Why that happens and what jargon like 'stocks' and 'debtors' means will be explained later.

For now, the key point is that profits will only keep the business going if they produce enough cash, and they will only do that if you have good financial control. In contrast, a concern making losses but which has reserves of cash can survive for as long as good financial control enables it to eke out that cash. Therefore it is just as important to plan for cash as it is for profit.

What is financial control?

Full financial control means:

- ☐ Knowing where you are now — annual accounts
- ☐ Planning where you are going — budgets
- ☐ Making sure you get there — progress reports and controls to check what's going on.

You cannot achieve all this at once. To begin, you need an understanding of what your annual accounts tell you about the business so that's where this book starts. Though the second stage is shown above as producing a budget, I deal first with some simple controls and progress reports. The reason is that you must have reliable and prompt information about the key facts of your current financial position before you can budget realistically. Even more to the point, you can do something about installing these controls and reports straight away — in fact they are in one sense more important than a budget because, until you have today under control, plans for tomorrow are likely to stay wishful thinking. Budgets are based upon the understanding that the first two parts of the book will give you.

Your accounts are a goldmine of facts

Your accounts contain valuable clues about the state of your business but poor presentation may make them difficult to unearth. Accounts do not talk — you must read them. Your records must first be organised so that they produce the right figures; then those figures must be interpreted and made to tell the story. To understand that story, not only do you need to be able to read a set of accounts but to understand how the numbers relate to each other. That's what you'll be shown in the next few chapters: where to look for the gold which is hidden under all that accountant's jargon.

The jargon will be explained, but I won't try to turn you into an accountant — just equip you with enough knowledge to understand your figures.

Why your accountant does not do this for you

Have you ever wished your accountant would do just what I am promising — and wondered why it did not happen? Well, it's your money, isn't it? (Even if you only run a part of someone else's business, they are your figures on which you are judged.) The interest must begin with *you*. Your accountant, whether an external auditor or an internal colleague, is a busy person. With many demands on his (or her) time, he'll naturally do most for the client or colleague who takes an informed interest in the figures he produces. Such a client is much easier to help than the one who has to be prodded into even looking at the numbers. Besides, the key to getting the best answers from any specialist is knowing the questions to ask.

That's the rub! You aren't sure of the questions or you would not be reading this, and most accountants are not very good at explaining finance to laymen anyway. To do so clearly is a skill requiring practice they often have not had. Most non-accountants have trouble with the financial aspects of business unless they are lucky enough to have at their elbow one of those rare accountants who are good at explaining the results of their labours. If finance troubles you too, this book will help you.

Chapter 2

The Ownership of a Business

If you know the difference between a sole trader, a partner and a director of a limited company just skim this section quickly to check for any points new to you. If you don't know, the following explanation will help you understand some of the later chapters.

A business can operate as a sole trader, a partnership, a limited company or as a cooperative. There are important legal and tax differences and each has advantages and disadvantages.

What is a sole trader?

A sole trader is an individual who works for himself though not necessarily alone; he may have employees. All the profits (or losses) are his and he pays income tax on them as an individual, though of course under the rules for business profits, not under Pay As You Earn (PAYE).

He may trade under his own name or one which describes it, such as Acme Window Cleaners. Sometimes, when a business is sold, the new owner retains the name of the previous owner.

What is a partnership?

A partnership is a group of two or more people who agree to share the risks, profits and losses of a business. They can agree whatever terms they wish as to who contributes what money or time to the business and how the profits are shared. Each partner, however, is responsible for all the debts incurred by the business. Each can therefore be made bankrupt should a creditor decide to claim from him because he has assets and his partners do not, or perhaps because they have even disappeared. Thus a partnership has no *legal* existence in its own right — it is just a group of individuals who agree to work together sharing not just premises, equipment, etc, but also the profits or losses resulting from their activities.

The partnership agreement can be verbal but it is much more sensible to put it in writing. A partnership can also trade under a different name from those of the partners. Each partner is taxed individually on his or her share of the partnership profits, as shown by the partnership accounts, under the income tax rules.

What is a limited company?

A limited company is a separate legal entity in its own right. It is governed by strict rules in the Companies Acts and it can only be set up after complying with various formalities.

It must file accounts with the Registrar of Companies each year which are open to public inspection. It is illegal to add the word 'Limited' to your trading name until your company has complied with the Registrar's requirements and he has issued a certificate of registration.

The reason for this formality is that 'limited' means limited liability for the shareholders. They can lose only the money that they have put into the company. This is in contrast with sole traders or partners who must use their private assets if necessary to meet the debts of their businesses and who can be made bankrupt for those debts.

Since a limited company is a legal entity in its own right, it can make contracts and can sue or be sued. Naturally the people running the company act on its behalf, but they cannot usually be held personally responsible for the results unless, of course, they have given personal guarantees. There are exceptions: a director can be held responsible for unpaid National Insurance contributions, for instance, and must not act recklessly or illegally.

A limited company pays corporation tax on its profits. It deducts PAYE from the pay of its employees, including the salaries of directors, and must pass that deduction on to the government like any other employer. The profits of a limited company belong to the shareholders, as explained below.

What is a cooperative?

A cooperative is an association of people who join together to achieve mutually agreed aims. They have equal standing in the business. The members are the shareholders. The cooperative may be set up as a partnership or a limited company, in which case the above comments apply. Cooperatives registered as cooperative societies are registered under the Industrial and Provident Societies Acts 1965–78 and the law is administered by the Registrar of Friendly Societies. They pay corporation tax and must file audited accounts annually with their Registrar.

A company goes on for ever

Unlike a sole trader, who can cease trading at will, or a partnership which can be dissolved, a company continues indefinitely. It only ceases to have a legal existence if its shareholders decide to close it down or if its creditors force it into liquidation because it has not paid their bills.

When the majority shareholder of a company dies, the company carries on, whereas if a sole trader dies, his business ceases in law and the assets pass to his heirs who begin a new business even if they continue trading the way he did. Of course, in the case of a one-man company there is little practical difference but the heirs inherit the shares in the company, not the actual assets of the business.

What are 'shareholders' and 'directors'?

The shareholders own the company. When the company is formed, they subscribe for shares in it (called share capital), paying for them either in cash or in assets. For instance, when a sole trader incorporates his business as a limited company, he receives shares in exchange for the equipment, goods, etc handed over to the company. Share capital is explained in more detail in Chapter 6.

The board of directors runs the business. Individual directors may or may not own shares in it but, in small businesses, the directors and shareholders are often the same people. The directors of a small company usually work full time in it.

In large companies, some of the directors may be 'non-executive'. These are not managers working full time in the business; they merely attend board meetings. They are really consultants or advisers and their fees are often much smaller than the salaries of the full-time directors.

Who controls the company — directors or shareholders?

In companies where they are not the same people, it is the directors who run the business. They are responsible for preparing the accounts which they must present to the shareholders each year for approval at the annual general meeting. There are also certain actions for which they have to obtain the approval of the shareholders, such as increases in the share capital.

Theoretically the shareholders of a major company can tell the directors what to do. Usually it is not practical for them to run the business of the company themselves — there may be many thousands of them for one thing — so this really means that they can vote new directors on to the board, who they think will run the business more to their liking than did the old ones.

In large companies the directors often hold a very small proportion of the shares. In practice they do not often get voted out by the shareholders unless they have run the business very badly or unless their conduct has been highly controversial and public opinion has been aroused.

Salaries for directors and dividends for shareholders

Directors are paid salaries or fees with deduction of PAYE and NI contributions, just like any other employee.

Shareholders receive dividends on their shares, if there are enough profits to pay them and if they decide to take a dividend. In small companies where they are the same people, directors often pay themselves salaries rather than take dividends. Earned income may have tax advantages compared with an unearned dividend. The 1984 Finance Act changed the rules and the removal of the ceiling for employers' NI contributions in 1985 increased the company's tax bill for high salaries, so dividends will now be more common — until the rules alter again!

Why trade as a limited company?

Many small companies are really only sole traders who have chosen to trade under limited liability. The practical trading differences, as opposed to legal ones, are few in such cases. Moreover, the advantages to the owner of limited liability for the debts of his business are often less than they seem at first sight.

Banks often demand either security or personal guarantees, or both, from the directors to cover an overdraft, while the Department of Health and Social Security can sue them for National Insurance contributions if the company fails to pay them over. In practice, therefore, the owners of a small business often obtain protection only from their suppliers, useful though that can be.

Limited liability can be helpful in trades which have a high failure rate, such as builders, or a high potential public liability, such as food or drug manufacturers.

Normally, limited liability also becomes a valuable advantage once the ordinary creditors become larger than the financial resources of the owners can repay. Being in business is never without risk and limited liability allows large businesses to function without the directors being personally involved in any losses. As explained below, it also allows outsiders to invest money in the business without having to manage it. Without the rules of limited liability, it would be impossible for big businesses to exist because the necessary finances can only be provided by outside shareholders. Individuals are not rich enough to own the big business which they run.

There can also be tax advantages in having a company in which the necessary cash reserves to finance it more easily can be built up if the tax rate is lower than you would pay as an individual. However, the profit figure at which that becomes true is often higher than is supposed. The position changes from time to time as governments alter the tax rules so advice from a good accountant is essential.

If a business grows too big for one man or a small number of partners to manage, incorporation also enables them to allow their employees a stake in the business by issuing shares to them. It can also be easier to pass on a limited company to the founder's children in the same way by giving them shares during his lifetime.

For many small businesses, however, there is not much advantage in becoming a limited company. There can be serious tax disadvantages if the owner(s) wish to take out cash which has accumulated in the company. Moreover, if partners incorporate their business but then fall out, the company cannot simply be divided up like the assets of a partnership. It has a legal existence of its own and dissolving it or buying out one of its shareholders can cause legal and tax problems, especially if relationships are bad.

Another serious disadvantage of a limited company is that it is subject to more red tape. It has to file accounts each year with the Registrar of Companies. Moreover, the layout of those accounts and the information shown in them are tightly regulated by the Companies Acts, supplemented by rules laid down by the professional accounting bodies. There are complex requirements designed to protect shareholders and creditors which are often meaningless for the small family-controlled company. They also cause high audit fees.

Whereas a sole trader or partnership needs accounts primarily to help run the business and to keep the tax man quiet, a company must have its accounts audited by a qualified professional accountant who must certify that they comply with the requirements; if they do not, he must say so and why. This means extra time complying with the rules even though the resulting information usually means nothing to the owner of a small company.

A good professional accountant is invaluable to the small business because of the advice he can offer but the extra cost of an audit certificate in the case of a company is bad news.

Do not confuse '& Co' with a limited company

The word 'company' is often loosely used in business. 'J Bloggs & Co' sounds more imposing than 'J Bloggs'. Sole traders or partnerships can add the words '& Co' to their trading names if they wish and this has no legal effect. However, when people talk of 'a company', they usually mean a 'limited' company as described above.

Can a small company raise money by issuing shares?

There is no reason why a small company should not issue shares to outsiders, but it is illegal to issue a prospectus to the public at large asking them to subscribe for shares, unless you first comply with certain rules.

However, the taxation rules have been altered to make it more attractive for investors to put money into the smaller company through the Business Expansion Scheme. This has resulted in a number of financial organisations promoting funds which accept money from investors for placing under the scheme. Whether these will succeed in making enough profits on their successes to cover the inevitable losses remains to be seen. The issue of shares to outsiders is not a practical proposition for most small businesses, if only because most of the owners dislike sharing the ownership of their business.

Summary

A business can be owned by either a sole trader, a partnership, a limited company or a cooperative (which can function as a partnership or a limited company). Sole traders are taxed on their profits under income tax as are partners on their share of the partnership profits. A company's profits are taxed under corporation tax though small companies run by their owners often pay out most of the profit as salaries to the directors. The profit is then subject to income tax in the hands of each director under the PAYE rules rather than left in the company to pay corporation tax.

Companies have to file accounts for public inspection whereas sole traders and partnerships do not. Moreover, the form these accounts take is strictly controlled and they are in consequence more expensive to produce.

The example of a set of accounts in Chapter 3 is for the sole trader — as the simplest situation. Later on we shall see what the accounts of a limited company look like — though I stress that this book is about accounts for use in managing your business. Little time is spent on details which are only there because the law says they must be, however small the company.

What Do Annual Accounts Consist of?

Annual accounts consist of a *profit and loss account* and a *balance sheet*. The profit and loss account shows what has happened during the year and whether the result is a profit or a loss; the balance sheet shows where the business has then got to, ie what it owns and what it owes — its assets and its liabilities.

These accounts state in formal terms what you no doubt do informally in managing your personal affairs. During the month you earn so much in salary, or draw so much from your business, and spend this on food, rent or mortgage, clothes, entertainment, beer etc. At the end of the month you add up what you have left. You may have some money left over; perhaps you have no cash left or you owe some to other people or to your bank. The point is that you need to know whether you have spent more or less money than you have earned in that month. This is your personal profit and loss account — a statement of what has happened during the month.

In summing up your affairs, you will take into account any exceptional spending on furniture or video equipment, for example, things that will be of use to you for some time ahead. You could even draw up a personal balance sheet. Most of your spending would have no further value to you, but things such as furniture, clothes and so on could be listed and a figure put on them. You could thus show whether your net worth in terms of things owned and money in the bank was greater or less at the end of the month than at the beginning.

The profit and loss account

You may also meet the terms 'trading account' and 'appropriation account' which are jargon for sections of the profit and loss account.

The profit and loss account shows the profit or loss made during the period covered (a month, quarter, year etc). This is after allowing for bills owed but not yet paid (creditors), amounts owed to the business but not yet received (debtors) and sums, such as rent, paid for periods not yet finished (payments in advance).

The balance sheet

The balance sheet shows the value of the business at the date to which the profit and loss account was made up. It lists the assets: buildings, equipment, stocks, debtors, cash etc — and the liabilities: loans, creditors, bank overdraft and so on. The difference between the two totals is the owner's interest in the business. If it is a limited company this is called share capital and reserves: if it is a partnership or a sole trader it is shown as partner's or owner's capital and current accounts.

The owner's interest is in fact the original cash put into the business, plus profits earned since after tax, less cash drawn out.

The next two chapters explain the profit and loss account and the balance sheet in detail, define the accounting jargon and show you which are the key figures and ratios. You do not have to learn all the accountancy language but you do need enough understanding of the more important terms to be able to read your accounts and discuss them with your accountant.

Who sees the accounts (apart from the owners or shareholders)?

Every business needs accounts in order to agree its tax liability. In addition, a limited company must file a copy of its accounts with the Registrar of Companies, and a cooperative with the Registrar of Friendly Societies, where they are available for public inspection.

The bank manager may ask to see a copy, particularly if he has lent money to the business. The VAT inspector also has the right to ask to see the accounts.

How often are accounts needed?

Normally accounts are prepared annually but this may vary. Progressive businessmen use their accounts to help them run their business. It is often helpful to have half-yearly, quarterly or even monthly accounts in order to provide up-to-date information on the business.

How frequently you need them depends on your business. In many cases, the small businessman does not need complete figures during the year. Provided he has an overall grasp of his annual results and he has projected a budget for the coming year, he can keep track of what is happening by comparing the key figures against his forecast. There are usually only two or three such figures, which alter from month to month, such as sales, purchase of goods for resale, and wages. Often he can keep track of these during the year without formal accounts.

That really only applies to the smallest businesses, however, and even they can benefit from, say, quarterly accounts. Without them, it is so easy for things to go wrong financially without your noticing. Producing regular accounts forces you to add up and make sense of the numbers. That often highlights horror stories before they have gone on long enough for the loss to be serious.

Questions

Check your answers with the text.

☐ What is the difference between a profit and loss account and a balance sheet?

☐ Does the profit and loss account show:
   (a)   the value of expenses incurred (ie commitments made), or
   (b)   those actually spent (cash paid out)?

Chapter 4

The Profit and Loss Account Explained

As mentioned in Chapter 3 the profit and loss account shows how much profit (or loss) you have made. The example on page 27 is of an account for a small shop. It starts with sales, deducts the cost of sales to show the gross profit, then deducts expenses to show the net profit (or loss). Each of these headings is explained below. Please read the notes in conjunction with the example.

'Last year' and 'this year'

The figures for last year are given to show how the results for this year (the year just ended) have changed. Often a comparison with the figure for last year is more useful in helping you to understand the progress of your business than looking at this year in isolation. Changes in figures reveal trends which can be compared with what you think ought to have happened, perhaps showing you where action is needed to correct a problem. If you cannot rationalise a change, something is probably wrong. That applies when a figure is better than you expected, ie income is higher or a cost is lower. Investigation could reveal a mistake — sometimes simple errors such as adding up incorrectly or putting an amount under the wrong heading are highlighted by comparisons with the previous period. Comparisons are one of the most useful techniques in looking at figures.

Sales (or takings or turnover) £249,560

This is the value of goods sold (or services provided in, say, a hair-dressing salon or a contracting business). It does not include VAT because that belongs to the government. It is net of any credits to customers for returns, discounts, etc, though these could be shown as a separate deduction if significant.

If you sell on credit, you count as sales the value of goods despatched or services performed during the period, *not* just the cash you have received.

THE XYZ SHOP
Profit and loss account for the year ended 30 June 19XX

Last year £				This year £
221,000	**Sales**			249,560
25,000	Opening stock (on 1 July last year)	27,000		
168,900	Add purchases	199,360		
193,900		226,360		
27,000	Less closing stock (on 30 June this year)	34,200		
166,900	**Cost of goods sold**			192,160
54,100	**Gross profit** 23% (24.5% last year)			57,400
11.200	Staff wages			12,500
7,400	Rent			7,400
4,100	Rates			4,600
2,700	Heat and light			3,000
550	Telephone			600
700	Insurance			800
950	Professional fees			1,000
1,700	Motor expenses			2,000
3,000	Advertising			3,200
1,300	Repairs			1,500
500	Stationery and postage			500
1,500	Sundry expenses			1,400
35,600	**Total expenses**			38,500
1,000	**Interest:** loan	1,000		
2,000	bank overdraft	2,500		3,500
3,400	**Depreciation:** equipment, fixtures and fittings	3,400		
2,500	motor vehicle	2,000		5,400
£9,600	**Net profit before tax**			£10,000
	The net profit can be re-stated as			
8,300	Proprietor's salary			9.200
1,300	'Super profit'			800
£9,600				£10,000

Cost of goods sold £192,160

From your sales, you must deduct the cost of providing or producing what you sell. This is called cost of goods sold and is the next figure down in the right-hand column.

Most accountants use the term 'cost of sales' rather than 'cost of goods sold'. Both terms mean the same but laymen usually understand the latter term more easily.

If you sell goods, your cost of goods sold is the cost to you of the items you sell. If you provide services, your cost of sales is any material you use. If you employ staff whose time you sell, such as in a repair workshop, your cost of sales may be mostly wages.

Cost of sales or cost of goods sold therefore means those of your costs which vary directly in proportion to your sales. In most businesses the only cost which varies directly with sales is goods purchased or produced.

You arrive at the value sold or used up in sales during the year by adding to the stock you held at the start the goods you purchased, and then deducting the stocks you have left. This calculation is inset in the left-hand column between 'sales' and 'cost of goods sold'. The figures are explained below.

Stocks — opening £27,000, closing £34,200

The stock figure is the value of the goods held for sale to customers or of materials held for use in performing your services.

Stocks are valued at cost net of VAT (valued added tax) *not* at selling price. If you valued them at selling price you would be taking profit on them before you had sold them. Any items which are old, obsolete, in poor condition or held in excessive quantities in relation to sales should be priced down to realistic values.

Purchases £199,360

This is the value of goods net of VAT received between the two stocktaking dates, *not* the total of cash paid to creditors. This is because, when you count stock, you list what you have. Thus it is the invoice for goods you have had in which must be shown as purchases. It is net of any returns to suppliers. Discounts received from suppliers may be shown separately if important.

Gross profit £57,400

This is a key figure. It is the profit per item sold or service rendered after charging your cost of sales but before paying all your fixed costs such as rent, rates, electricity etc. Since your cost of goods sold should be roughly constant as a percentage of sales, so should your gross profit.

Gross profit is very important. If you do not have the right profit at the gross level, you cannot have it at the net. Suppose gross profit is 25 per cent of sales and net profit 10 per cent, a 1 per cent variation from 25 to 24 per cent looks trivial — it's only 4 per cent of your gross profit: but the same 1 per cent becomes 10 per cent of your net profit (1 per cent on 10 per cent).

In practice gross profit is never a constant percentage of sales, for various reasons. For example, as your sales rise you should obtain better buying terms; on the other hand, stock losses can make a large hole in your profit.

Some causes of stock losses are:

☐ damaged goods destroyed or sold off at lower prices
☐ natural losses by evaporation etc
☐ inaccurate measuring of quantities sold or pricing errors
☐ human errors by you in invoicing where goods are sold on credit or by supplier when bought on credit
☐ fraud by customers (shoplifting etc)
☐ fraud by suppliers (wrong deliveries or inaccurate invoicing)
☐ fraud by staff (cash or goods taken; goods supplied to friends at wrong prices etc)

See Chapter 9 for more about gross profit.

Expenses (wages and other overheads as listed in the example) £38,500

These are the expenses of operating the business for the period. In some cases, such as wages, the cost is usually the same as cash paid out. But for bills, such as telephone bills, which are incurred on credit, the cost for the period is the bills which relate to that period, *not* just those which happen to have been paid during it.

Similarly, some expenses are paid in advance. Rent, rates and insurance are examples, and for these, the cost is the proportion relating to the period of the accounts, not the total paid out.

Depreciation £5,400

Depreciation is a different sort of cost from the other expenses: there is no invoice in the books for it but it is a cost none the less. Many assets used in the business wear out over a period. Plant, equipment, fixtures, fittings and vehicles are examples. These are not written off when they are bought. Their cost is shown in the balance sheet, as explained in the next chapter under fixed assets. The objective of depreciation is to charge against profits the cost of the asset over its working life. When it is either sold or scrapped, the depreciation charged up to that date therefore represents profit set aside to replace it.

Note that the profit set aside may not be represented by actual cash. The cash may already have been used to finance other fixed assets, stocks, debtors etc. The reasons why profit is not necessarily the same as cash will become clearer as you read subsequent chapters.

Note also that since estimates or averages have to be used for each kind of asset, the amount is only an intelligent guess, not a precise forecast.

The depreciation is based upon historic cost. The price of a replacement item may have risen substantially due to inflation, technological advances etc. So you might need to make extra provision for the replacement of assets over and above normal depreciation.

See the comment about fixed assets in the next two chapters for more about different methods of calculating depreciation.

Net profits before tax £10,000

I re-state this as you can see in the example. Proprietor's (or director's) salary represents the wage of the owner manager. When looking at how you are doing, make a realistic estimate of what you could earn in a job. Only if there is a surplus are you earning a 'super profit' which is the real return you obtain from your investment in the business. It is the correct figure to compare with the return you could obtain by selling the business, investing the proceeds and taking a job. Express your 'super profit' as a percentage of your interest in the business and you have the real reward for all the extra sweat of being the boss.

See Chapters 9 and 10 for more comments on how the fall in gross profit has hit the real return earned by the owner of this business, reducing it to a miserable figure.

Questions

Check your answers with the text.

☐ Does the sales figure include VAT?
☐ Does the stock valuation include VAT?
☐ Is the purchases figure:
  (a)   value of goods received in the period, or
  (b)   value of invoices received in the period, or
  (c)   total of cash paid to suppliers in the period?
☐ What does the cost of goods sold figure represent?
☐ What are the causes of stock losses? (Give at least five.)
☐ What is gross profit?

Chapter 5

The Balance Sheet Explained

Now we come to the second statement which makes up a set of accounts — the balance sheet.

Read this chapter in conjunction with the example for the XYZ shop on page 27. If you own or work for a limited company, you will also need to read Chapter 6 on the accounts of a limited company, since there are differences between the accounts for sole traders or partnerships and those of limited companies. Read this one first, however, because various points are common to all businesses.

As already explained in Chapter 3, the balance sheet shows where the business has got to at the date on which the profit and loss account ends. It is, if you like, a snapshot of the business at that moment. In contrast, the profit and loss account can be likened to a video of the events during the year. The example begins with what the business owns, its assets, and deducts its liabilities, to arrive at the net value, the proprietor's interest; sometimes, however, the latter (for a limited company the share capital) is shown at the top.

There are three kinds of assets: fixed, intangible and current.

Fixed assets

These are the items which the business buys to retain for use over a long period, rather than to resell at a profit. They are usually kept until they wear out, become obsolete or are no longer suitable for the business. Examples are buildings, plant, equipment, fixtures and fittings and vehicles. The layout shown here for fixed assets is that usually adopted for sole traders or partnerships (for limited companies, see Chapter 6). The details, for convenience, are shown in the balance sheet in the example, but they are usually in a separate note. The net book value is the balance remaining after deducting, from the NBV at the start of the year, the depreciation as shown in the profit and loss account. Additions and sales of assets during the year are also shown and the depreciation is calculated for a full year on the starting net book value after deducting any sales, and proportionately on items bought during the year. This is called the 'reducing balance' method of depreciating and, since a percentage

THE XYZ SHOP
Balance sheet at 30 June 19XX
(vertical layout)

Last year		Net book value of start of year	Bought in year	Sales in year	Depreciation for year	This year Net book value end of year
£	**Fixed assets**	£	£	£	£	£
11,000	Equipment	11,000	3,000	200	2,400	11,400
10,000	Fixtures	10,000	—	—	1,000	9,000
8,000	Vehicle	8,000	—	—	2,000	6,000
29,000		29,000	3,000	200	5,400	26,400
3,000	**Goodwill**					3,000
	Current assets					
27,250	Stock (trade £34,200: other £300)				34,500	
5,500	Accounts receivable (debtors)				6,000	
950	Payments in advance				1,000	
33,700						41,500
65,700	**Total assets**					70,900
	Less:					
	Current liabilities due within one year					
7,500	Accounts payable (creditors)				9,000	
1,800	Future tax payable				2,000	
16,000	Bank overdraft				18,000	
25,300						29,000
	Creditors due after one year					
10,000	Loan					10,000
£30,400	**Proprietor's interest in the business**					31,900
	Represented by:					
29,000	Balance of capital at start of year					30,400
7,700	Add profit for year (after tax of £2,000)					8,000
36,700						38,400
6,300	Deduct drawings					6,500
£30,400	**Balance of capital at end of year**					£31,900

of the reducing total is written off, the assets are never fully depreciated. It is simple to use, and it is not necessary to keep records of each item in order to show when it is written off. An alternative, the 'straight line' method, is explained in Chapter 6.

Intangible assets

These include goodwill, patent, trade-mark or royalty rights and other items for which cash is paid but which have no tangible form.

Goodwill

In the example, the proprietor of the business paid £3,000 for goodwill when he bought it. That is to say, the price he paid exceeded by £3,000 the value of the net assets he took over. Net assets are fixtures and fittings, equipment, stock, debtors etc, less any liabilities to creditors etc, for which he accepted responsibility.

People are often confused about goodwill. It is not an identifiable asset with its own value. It is in effect a balancing figure arrived at as follows.

Say you are offered a business earning a net profit of £12,000. You are prepared to pay 1½ years' profits for it, plus stock at valuation. You are therefore buying the leasehold, fixed assets and goodwill for £18,000. If the fixed assets are valued at £14,000 you are paying £4,000 for the right to the leasehold (not usually separated from goodwill) and the goodwill. If any debtors or creditors were taken over they would, of course, be a part of the calculation.

However, the value of the fixed assets always depends upon the view you take of them. If you value them for use as they stand in a going concern, they are worth far more than if you tried to sell them off as surplus. So the balancing figure taken as the value of goodwill is arbitrary. One cannot value goodwill for itself — only as a consequence of deciding what one will pay for a given amount of profit and then deducting one's valuation of fixed assets and current assets, if applicable, from the price paid.

Current assets

These are the items arising and constantly changing in the course of trading. Examples are stocks which convert into debtors which become cash. Note that 'other' stocks are such items as stationery or fuel. 'Trade' stocks are goods for resale or for use in manufacturing other goods.

Long-term liabilities

Liabilities are long term or short term. Long-term liabilities are amounts repayable more than a year ahead such as loans, mortgages etc; but *not* a bank overdraft because this is repayable on demand.

Current liabilities

These are amounts repayable within one year such as creditors, bank overdrafts, short-term loans etc.

Accounts receivable or payable (debtors and creditors)

A debtor owes you money. You owe money to a creditor. It may help you to distinguish between them if you recall that it is the creditors of a business who force it into liquidation. One talks of a creditors' winding up, not a debtors' one.

More about stocks

For a retailer or wholesaler, stocks consist of the goods he deals in. A manufacturer often has various kinds of stock such as:

- ☐ raw materials
- ☐ bought-in parts and sub-assemblies
- ☐ work in progress
- ☐ finished goods
- ☐ stationery, advertising and sales promotion materials, fuel etc.

These are explained below.

Raw materials
One man's finished goods are another man's raw materials. Raw materials are those goods which a business buys in order to transform them by its production processes into finished products. Examples are the timber, nails, glue etc bought by a furniture manufacturer or the powders, perfumes and chemicals used by a cosmetics manufacturer.

Bought-in parts
Many businesses buy in parts for use in assembling their products. For instance, the cosmetics manufacturer buys in jars and pots in which to put his lotions and creams and the car manufacturer purchases sparking plugs for his engines. Such parts are often distinguished from raw materials by being called bought-in parts, components or even sub-assemblies.

Sub-assemblies are sections of a product put together by a supplier specifically for the manufacturer. A car manufacturer, for instance, might buy in complete door handle and window winding assemblies for his car doors.

Sub-assemblies may also be sections of a product put together by the manufacturer himself and awaiting the next stage in the production process. In this case they will very likely be classified as work in progress.

Work in progress

Work in progress stocks are those which are part-way through the production cycle. For example, a motor vehicle is assembled through various stages. Since the production process is continuous, there are bound to be unfinished vehicles are the date of taking stock.

The term 'work in progress' is also used to describe work done on unfinished construction contracts. In a service industry or a professional office such as that of an accountant or an architect, work in progress is the time spent on jobs which have not yet been charged to the customer or the client because the work is incomplete.

Finished goods (or, in the USA, 'inventory')

Finished goods are stocks ready for sale to customers. This does not necessarily mean that they are goods which the ultimate customer would recognise. The sub-assembly bought by a car manufacturer for his car door is 'finished goods' to the business which makes it, even though it is several stages away from the state in which the car reaches the showroom.

Stationery, advertising and sales promotion materials, heating fuel etc

These goods are overhead expenses of most businesses rather than part of the direct cost of goods bought or produced for resale. Expenditure on them is shown in the profit and loss account as an expense, not as part of cost of sales.

Sales promotional materials are items such as sales brochures, catalogues, sales stands for shop counters, and so on.

Once incurred, an expense normally has no residual value, unlike a production cost which produces stock. Often, therefore, stocks of stationery, advertising and sales promotion materials, fuel etc, are ignored. If the value of such stocks is significant, however, they can be counted and included in the balance sheet. This is often done if a large bill has been incurred just before the end of the financial year for goods which will mostly be used during the following year.

The charge to the expense heading in the profit and loss account is then the total of bills received for the goods in question less the value of the stocks carried forward to the next accounting period (plus any stocks brought forward from the previous accounting period).

Proprietor's interest in the business

This represents the cash originally put in plus profits, less taxation

THE BALANCE SHEET EXPLAINED

THE XYZ SHOP
Balance sheet at 30 June 19XX
(horizontal layout)

Last year	Capital	This year
£		£
29,000	Balance of capital at start of year	30,400
7,700	Add profit for year (after tax of £2,000)	8,000
		38,400
36,700		
6,300	Deduct drawings	6,500
30,400	**Proprietor's interest in the business**	31,900
10,000	**Creditors due after one year**	
	Loan	10,000
	Current liabilities due within one year	
7,500	Accounts payable (creditors)	9,000
1,800	Future tax payable	2,000
16,000	Bank overdraft	18,000
25,300		29,000
£65,700		£70,900

Last year	Fixed assets	Net book value start of year	Bought in year	Sales in year	Depreciation for year	This year Net book value end of year
£		£	£	£	£	£
	Equipment	11,000	3,000	200	2,400	11,400
	Fixtures	10,000	—	—	1,000	9,000
	Vehicle	8,000	—	—	2,000	6,000
29,000		29,000	3,000	200	5,400	26,400
3,000	Goodwill					3,000
	Current assets					
27,250	Stock (trade £34,200: other £300)					34,500
5,500	Accounts receivable (debtors)					6,000
950	Payments in advance					1,000
33,700						41,500
£65,700						£70,900

and drawings and any losses. In the balance sheet of a limited company it is shown as share capital and reserves, the total of which belongs to the shareholders. Individual directors, who may or may not be the shareholders, may have amounts owing to them on current account as well but these sums are current liabilities. 'Drawings' of profit for a company are dividends to the shareholders. If the directors own the company, they may of course draw profit as salaries rather than as dividends.

In a partnership, and sometimes for a sole trader, a distinction is made between permanent capital and current account balances of profits not drawn. The total of capital and current balances is then the proprietor's interest.

Expressed slightly differently, the owner's interest is the value of what the business owns less what it owes to outsiders.

'Vertical' or 'horizontal' layout

The proprietor's interest is a liability of the business to him. This is why, in a 'horizontal' layout of a balance sheet, it appears in the liabilities. The same figures used for the sample 'vertical' balance sheet are re-laid out as in the 'horizontal' layout shown because some accountants use this form.

Questions

Check your answers with the text.

☐ What are:
   (a) fixed assets
   (b) intangible assets and goodwill
   (c) current assets
   (d) long-term liabilities
   (e) current liabilities
   (f) proprietor's interest in the business?
☐ What kinds of stock are there? (Five are discussed.)

Chapter 6

The Accounts of a Limited Company

This chapter discusses how the accounts of a small limited company differ from those of a sole trader or a partnership. In Chapter 2 I explained the legal distinctions which the accounts reflect. We'll discuss the accounts of big companies later in the book. At present we are looking at the figures for a small business which happens to be a limited company, ABC Ltd. You will need to have read Chapters 4 and 5 because many of the headings are the same and I comment only on the differences.

The profit and loss account

This book explains the figures in your accounts which you can use in running your business; it is not primarily concerned with the formalities of presentation which the law requires. But when you start to read an actual set of accounts, you will find they are more complicated than my examples, because all limited companies, big or small, are subject to rules in the Companies Acts as to the information which they must show in their accounts.

The example of a profit and loss account in Chapter 4 shows the detailed information which is included in the management accounts for a small business if it produces its own figures. If the accounts are done by professional accountants, as they often are for small companies owned by their directors, a detailed profit and loss account is included in the copies for the owners. The accounts sent to the Registrar of Companies will omit it, however.

In the published accounts for the Registrar and outside shareholders, if there are any, the profit and loss account has only to give certain figures, such as sales, cost of sales, totals for certain headings, such as selling and administration expenses and various specific costs, including salaries and wages, interest and the audit fee. In practice, much of this information is given in notes rather than in the profit and loss account or the balance sheet itself.

Very small companies can choose a simplified presentation for the figures, which they send to the Registrar of Companies, giving even fewer details.

You need to know all this only so that you are not confused when you try to compare these examples with a real set of accounts, which will seem much more complex. It isn't really, once you understand the idea, and you should find you can follow the presentation required by law when you have got the feel of mine.

Some differences in the figures for a company
The profit and loss account for a company differs from the example for a sole trader, which we have already looked at, in two important ways. First, the directors, being employees of the company, are paid salaries. This expense is shown either with or adjacent to the staff costs for other employees.

Thus the figure of profit shown below is after paying the directors whereas, for a sole trader, the profit is before his drawings — all the profit belongs to him. In the case of a company, the profit belongs to the shareholders, who may not be the same people as the directors. Hence the need to charge the latter's pay before arriving at the profit before tax. Second, there may be a dividend paid to the shareholders.

£			£
24,000	Net profit before tax		30,000
9,000	Less corporation tax		10,000
15,000	Net profit after tax		20,000
1,000	Less preference dividend		1,000
	Ordinary dividend interim already paid	£3,000	
6,500	final proposed	£6,000	9,000
7,500	Balance of profit undistributed for year		10,000
21,500	Add balance brought forward from previous years		29,000
£29,000	Balance of profit undistributed carried forward (see balance sheet)		£39,000

This example assumes that there are outside shareholders in the company who require dividends on their shares. If the shareholders are all directors, they may prefer to draw the profits as directors' salaries, rather than dividends, for tax reasons. Shares are explained later and dividends in the next chapter.

In this example, the company has a profit of £20,000 available after tax for distribution to shareholders or for retention in the company. Dividends either paid or proposed take £10,000, leaving £10,000 retained to add to the accumulated balance of previous retentions.

Is the profit retention of £10,000 cash in the bank?
Retained profits are not necessarily cash in the bank. The money may well have been used already to finance increased stocks or receivables (debtors), as is the case in this example. The company has an overdraft, as we shall see from the balance sheet a little further on. The reason for this is explained in later chapters.

How much profit should be retained?
Profit is not available to be taken out of a business until it results in cash in the bank. Even then you must leave money in your business to finance it, especially if your sales are growing, and you must build up resources for a rainy day.

The need to retain the profit varies from company to company and, to some extent, from trade to trade. Some industries, particularly manufacturers, have to invest more heavily in new equipment and require more working capital to finance stock or debtors in order to stay in business than do others. More sales mean more stock and more credit to customers which absorbs cash. This is further explained in later chapters.

Industries such as the furniture, building and construction industries tend to be cyclical, with good and bad years succeeding each other, as the economy changes. Such companies cannot pay out a high proportion of profits as dividends in good years if they are to maintain the dividend in poor ones. They tend, therefore, to retain a high proportion of profit in the good years to provide a cushion for the bad times when they may have difficulty in earning enough to 'cover' the dividend.

A few industries, such as retailing, tend to pay out a higher proportion of profit because they are more static. The business is more stable and swings in profits are less violent. If the company is well run, much of a retailer's working capital is provided by credit from his suppliers. A good proportion of his stocks can be sold for cash before or around the date on which he has to pay for them. He can therefore afford to pay out a higher proportion of profits and indeed often needs to do so because the attraction of his shares to an investor is more likely to be a secure steady income than the prospect of rapidly increasing profits.

Of course, the best companies in an industry tend to be exceptions to such general statements. Equally the financial situation of the company often dictates the policy. It may be necessary to plough back more profit than usual for several years to finance expansion. On the other hand, a high dividend may have to be paid in order to persuade the shareholders to invest fresh capital to pay for expansion because there is no way that the company can generate enough cash from its existing business.

The balance sheet

The example in this section is similar in outline to that of a sole trader or partnership but there are various differences in detail.

What is share capital?

It will help you to understand these notes if we deal first with share capital. It is not the first figure in the example but, since you must know what it is in order to follow the points made about other entries, it is dealt with first. So we start with the shareholders' interest.

Share capital — ordinary shares £15,000

As explained in Chapter 2 a company issues 'shares' as a receipt for the money put in by its shareholders. These shares can be sold by one shareholder to another or to a third party either privately, or, if the shares are 'quoted', through the Stock Exchange.

Sometimes shares are issued in return for assets transferred to the company rather than for cash paid into its bank account.

If the company is a private one, the transfer of its shares is often subject to control by the directors who have power to refuse to register the transfer to a person of whom they do not approve.

Instead of shares, the word 'stock' is sometimes used. Ordinary stock means the same thing as ordinary shares; do not confuse this with loan stock, which means a loan on fixed interest terms.

The ordinary shares usually control the company with one vote per share but there are sometimes different classes of ordinary share with different voting rights. Often these special shares are called 'A' shares. They may have no votes at all or they could have, say, ten times as many as the rest of the shares. The voting rights are fixed as part of the terms on which they are offered to shareholders and the reason for different rights is usually to preserve the status quo of control of the company.

The significance of voting rights is that he who controls over 50 per cent of the votes controls the company and can appoint the directors. For complete control, over 90 per cent of the votes is needed. The Companies Acts lay down different percentages which are needed to do different things such as change voting rights, repay share

ABC Limited
Balance sheet at 30 June 19XX

Last year £		Original cost £	Accumulated depreciation £	This year Net book value £
	Fixed assets			
30,400	Equipment	34,000	7,000	27,000
9,000	Fixtures and fittings	10,000	2,000	8,000
12,000	Vehicles	16,000	8,000	8,000
51,400		60,000	17,000	43,000
	Patents and trademarks			10,000
3,000	**Goodwill**			3,000
17,000	**Investment in associated company**			17,000
	Current assets			
50,000	Stocks (trade £65,000: other £3,000)		68,000	
9,000	Accounts receivable (debtors)		10,000	
2,600	Payments in advance		3,000	
61,600				81,000
133,000	**Total assets**			154,000
	Less:			
	Current liabilities due within one year			
12,000	Accounts payable (creditors)		13,000	
9,000	Current tax payable		8,000	
3,500	Ordinary dividend due (final only)		6,000	
23,500	Bank overdraft		30,000	
48,000				57,000
11,000	**Deferred taxation**			13,000
	Creditors due after one year			
10,000	Loan			10,000
£64,000	**Shareholders' interest in the business**			£74,000
	Represented by:			
	Share capital and reserves			
15,000	Ordinary shares of £1 (authorised £20,000)			15,000
10,000	10% preference shares of £1			10,000
10,000	Capital reserve			10,000
29,000	Balance of undistributed profit			39,000
£64,000				£74,000

capital etc, but 51 per cent gives control of the day-to-day management of the business.

What is authorised capital?

Shares can be issued at any time in return for money, or for an asset acquired by the company, up to the limit of its authorised capital. Once the authorised limit has been reached, the shareholders must approve any increase in it. Such an increase then remains available for issue as required. Thus, in the example, the company has an authorised capital of £20,000 but has only issued £15,000 of it.

Share capital is not cash

This is not to say that the company has £5,000 spare cash. When they authorise a given figure of share capital, the shareholders merely fix a limit upon the powers of the directors. No value is received by the company until it actually issues the shares.

Preference shares £10,000

A company sometimes has preference shares as well as ordinary shares. Preference shares are entitled only to a fixed percentage dividend — 10 per cent in the example (based on their nominal value — not on the value quoted on the Stock Exchange or elsewhere). The dividend is only payable if the directors consider that the profits (and cash position) are adequate but it ranks in priority before any dividend on the ordinary shares. Normally preference shares have no votes but often they obtain them if their dividend is not paid and this can result in the control of the company changing hands, depending upon the respective voting rights of the ordinary and preference shares.

Some preference dividends are cumulative until all arrears are cleared. Others are non-cumulative and the dividends are lost if not paid for any year.

If the company is wound up, the preference shares rank before the ordinary shares for repayment up to their nominal value. They can, however, be repaid without winding up the company if a majority of the holders agree; the ordinary shares, on the other hand, can only be repaid if the company is either wound up or reconstructed, which is a complicated legal process.

What does 'nominal value' of loan stock and ordinary shares mean?

The nominal value of loan stock or of ordinary shares is the figure which appears in the balance sheet of the issuing company and represents the amount it owes to the holders. In the case of loan stock or preference shares, this is the amount repayable as and when the stock is redeemed or the shares are repaid.

In the case of ordinary shares, however, nominal value is merely the original value fixed for the shares. Since the ordinary shareholders are entitled to the profits remaining after paying all fixed interest and preference dividends, it follows that, should the company be sold or wound up, the ordinary shareholders receive the net proceeds remaining after meeting all other obligations. This may be greater or less than the nominal value of their shares, depending on whether the company has made a profit or loss since the shares were issued. If the company is forced into liquidation by its creditors, the shareholders often receive nothing.

What is the actual value of shares?

The nominal value of shares, both ordinary and preference and of loan stock, has little bearing on their value if sold by one investor to another. The price obtainable, whether on the Stock Exchange or elsewhere, depends upon investors' expectations as to the income obtainable, the security of it, the possibility, for ordinary shares, of its increasing in the future and their assessment of the investment in comparison with the rates of return available elsewhere.

If a shareholding is large enough to justify a directorship for the holder, this increases its value, particularly in the case of a private company. The holder of 51 per cent of the shares of the private company can often largely ignore the wishes of the minority holders and in consequence, the latter's shares may be very difficult to sell at anything near the value per share of the majority holding.

Reserves — capital £10,000; profit and loss £39,000

A capital reserve is a profit on a capital asset, such as property. It is not always realised. An unrealised profit results from revaluing assets up from cost to the estimated present value. An actual sale produces a realised profit.

A capital reserve is not usually distributed by way of dividend. Indeed there are legal restrictions on doing so. For one thing the profit must be a realised one. Anyway, the money is often needed to finance the business.

A revenue reserve is available for distribution. It represents the balance of profits earned in previous years but not distributed. Often it is really the additional funds needed to let the company grow, and is permanent capital just as much as the share capital or capital reserves. If that is so, the cash is not available to pay out because it is tied up in stocks or other assets.

The difference between a reserve and a provision

A reserve is part of the shareholders' funds and represents profit tucked away to help finance the company and in case of a rainy day. A provision is an amount set aside to meet a specific liability. One example is the provision for deferred taxation explained later; another is a provision for bad debts which is an amount deducted from the profits in anticipation that some customers will not pay up.

Having explained the items which make up the shareholders' interest, we now go back to the example on page 42.

Fixed assets £60,000 – £17,000 = £43,000

Company law requires the original cost of the assets to be shown. This is therefore the first column in the example. The second column shows the accumulated depreciation written off to date for the years in which the assets have been owned. The third column shows the net book value of £43,000.

These totals cannot, of course, show any additions or sales during the year and the total values of any such changes have to be given in a separate note to the accounts. The accumulated depreciation figure includes the charge for the year shown in the profit and loss account.

Depreciation for a limited company is usually charged on the 'straight line' basis. Thus, a charge of 25 per cent on the original cost will write off an item over four years. This is in contrast to, say, 33⅓ per cent on the reducing balance, which, although a higher percentage, never completely writes it off, as explained in the comment on fixed assets in Chapter 5.

Office equipment, machinery etc is usually depreciated over ten years, except for computers which become obsolete so quickly that as little as three years may be appropriate. Cars are normally written off over four years: even though they are expected to fetch a substantial proportion of their original price when sold, second-hand prices fluctuate considerably and, as the replacement is sure to cost more than the old vehicle did, it is wise to write off too much rather than too little.

The cost of any leases of buildings has to be written off over the remaining period of the lease. This also applies to expenditure on fixtures and fittings which will not be removable if you have to vacate the premises. Freehold buildings are also supposed to be depreciated now following a recommendation by the professional accounting bodies. However, this is contentious and only public companies are likely to do so, usually at 2 per cent per annum.

If an item has been sold, the difference between the net book value and the price obtained will be shown in the profit and loss account as a profit (or loss) on sale of fixed assets. If the item has been scrapped, the whole of the net book value is a loss unless, of course, it was already fully depreciated and therefore in the books at a net value of nil. The most frequent such figure to appear is the profit or loss on the sale of a motor vehicle.

To use the straight line method accurately, the records of the company must show the total additions separately for each year so that after, say, ten years at 10 per cent, the additions for 1975 are no longer depreciated in 1985. Provided that one knows when an item was bought, it is then easy to calculate how much depreciation has been charged by the year in which it is sold, or scrapped. Even if the original cost is not known, it can be estimated and the totals for original cost and accumulated depreciation adjusted to reflect the sale. Without such figures year by year, one cannot tell how much of the assets is fully written off.

Plant registers help to keep track of fixed assets

Vehicles are easy to keep track of but individual machines and equipment can become merged as part of general plant, particularly if moved about. Many companies therefore number plant and keep a plant register so as to identify individual items as to age, specification, cost etc.

Without such a register, it can be difficult to identify the original cost of an item, which has to be taken out of the fixed assets total when it is sold. After a few years, it becomes impossible to reconcile the total in the balance sheet with the individual assets owned. Plant registers are therefore important in the larger company as an aid to keeping tabs on what the business owns.

Patents and trade marks

The company has acquired some patents and trade marks during the last year. The £10,000 cost could either be the purchase price or the expenses incurred if the company has designed and registered its own patent or mark.

Investment in associated company £17,000

An associated company is one in which the investing company effectively has a say in the management policy and has a director on the other company's board either because it is a partner or because it owns at least 20 per cent of the shares.

Since the investing company can influence the dividends paid to it, the investment is distinguished as 'associated' rather than 'trade'. Both 'associated' and 'trade' investments are held for the longer term but shares can also be held as a short-term home for spare funds, in which case they are treated as a current asset rather than separated, as here.

The investment in an associated company might include the cost of buying shares in it or long-term loans made to it. Any sums due from it for ordinary sales to it, or payable to it for ordinary purchases from it, on normal trade terms, are shown as 'amounts due from (or to) associated companies' in current assets or current liabilities. Under company law, such sums 'in the family' must not be hidden away in ordinary debtors or creditors.

Investments in subsidiary companies

A subsidiary company is one in which your company owns more than half the shares. It therefore controls it for practical purposes. There is no such investment in the example. Companies invest in other companies for many reasons, such as to diversify activities by starting new ones or buying existing operations, to defend themselves against their competitors or to form an alliance with suppliers or customers.

Goodwill was explained in Chapter 5.

Current tax payable £8,000

This is the tax due shortly as opposed to the provision for deferred taxation (see below).

Ordinary dividend due £6,000

This is the final dividend. The interim dividend was paid during the year as a payment on account. The directors can pay an interim dividend if they are satisfied that profits will cover it, but the final one needs approval by the shareholders at the annual general meeting.

Deferred taxation £13,000

Company tax law in the UK used to allow many companies to postpone the payment of a large part of their tax bills. This was the effective result of allowing them to write off 100 per cent of many (but not all) items of capital expenditure in the year in which tax was incurred. As a result, large provisions for deferred taxation were created to provide for the future liability in order to even out the tax bill.

Following changes in the rules made by the Finance Act 1984, 100 per cent write-off for tax in the first year will not be allowed so deferred tax provisions will be much smaller in future — at least until some future government changes the rules again!

Does your company have departmental accounts?

A substantial company may well have a number of different departments or activities. It will want to know how its sales, expenses and profits compare for these and its accounts may therefore be in several sections. However many different operating statements there may be in your company, you will see that they build up to a similar overall statement as shown in the earlier example even though much of the detail is on departmental schedules.

Questions

Check your answers with the text.

- [ ] What items does one find in a profit and loss appropriation account?
- [ ] What governs how much profit a business needs to retain?
- [ ] What is the meaning of the following:
  share capital
  authorised capital
  preference shares
  investments in associated companies?
- [ ] What is the difference between current and deferred tax?

Chapter 7

How the Figures in the Profit and Loss Account are Arrived at

The sum shown for each item in the profit and loss account is the amount of income earned or expense incurred during the period. This is a simple idea to grasp in theory, but do you understand what it means in practice? Here are three examples. The answers follow.

Sales

If all your sales are for cash — that is to say, if your customers hand over money (or a cheque) when you give them the goods or service — the total of your sales is the cash received.

But if you allow credit to your customers, is the sales figure:

(a) the total value of the goods and services which you deliver to them in the period (the value of any deliveries not yet invoiced being estimated)?
(b) the total of the invoices which you issue to them in the period?
(c) the total cash you receive from customers in the period?

Purchase of goods for resale

If your suppliers allow you credit, is the value of your purchases:

(a) the value of goods received from suppliers in the period (the value of any deliveries not yet invoiced being estimated)?
(b) the value of the invoices received from suppliers in the period?
(c) the total of cash paid to suppliers in the period?

Expenses

An 'expense' is an item of cost incurred in running a business, such as rent, rates, telephone etc, as opposed to goods bought for resale to customers.

For example, is the cost of the telephone:

(a) the value of the bills received in the period?
(b) the value of bills received as adjusted by an estimate for any period not covered by invoices to hand?
(c) the total cash paid to the telephone service?

For both sales and purchases (a) and (b) may be the same figures but this depends on whether your own and your suppliers' invoicing is up to date. The longer you wait before closing your records for the period, the fewer any missing invoices will be.

Try to work out the answers before you read on.

Answers
The answers are (a), (a) and (b). Here's why.

It is a common mistake to think of money as being earned or spent when the payment is made: in fact, this is often just the settlement of a sale which was achieved or a debt which was incurred much earlier.

The bank account shows the money coming in and the money going out, but this is no guide to the profit. To show the true position, we must allow for sales and liabilities for which we have not yet received the cash or for which we have not yet paid.

When is a sale a sale?

If you sell services, it is the date of the invoice to the customer which determines the accounting period into which the sale goes. All services provided up to the end of each period must either be invoiced or their value to date estimated as 'work in progress'. If you sell goods, the sale is made when they are delivered to the customer.

Sometimes a contract provides for progress payments prior to delivery. Credit for the sale is usually then taken in stages rather than on delivery though this depends upon the nature of the contract.

Watch your 'cut off' of goods against invoice

If you sell goods on credit, you must match the despatch of the goods with the invoices you issue. You would be taking a double profit if the goods were to be counted in stock and invoices for them also included in the sales. All goods which are despatched by the end of the accounting period must therefore be invoiced and included in your total of accounts receivable (debtors); conversely, goods still held are counted as stock and the invoice is dated in the following period in which they are actually despatched.

This procedure is sometimes called the 'cut off' because it determines the point at which you stop invoicing for one period and start for the next. The same procedure works in reverse for purchases of goods for resale.

When is a purchase a purchase?

Goods received before stock-taking will be included in the value of stocks counted: therefore the corresponding liability to the supplier must be included in accounts payable (creditors).

On the other hand, we do not want to include any suppliers' invoices in accounts payable unless the goods have been counted in stock.

This can only be done accurately if the suppliers' delivery notes are marked with the dates of receipt of the goods. Subsequently, these documents are matched with the invoices received from suppliers. It is sometimes necessary to estimate the value of invoices outstanding at the end of the accounting period in cases where suppliers are very slow to invoice.

Conversely, the date of receipt of any goods received after stock-taking should be marked on the delivery notes so as to prevent the invoices being included in accounts payable. The invoice belongs to the following accounting period because the goods have not been counted in stock.

This procedure for ensuring that invoices for goods bought are charged to the correct accounting period is especially important because the sums of money involved are often large in relation to other figures in the accounts. If the 'cut off' is wrong the profit margin percentage may well be seriously distorted. If this is not realised, the accounts may be misleading and cause wrong decisions to be taken.

Example
Suppose the stock includes goods received just before stock-taking to the value of £1,000, for which no corresponding invoice is included in accounts payable. As a result, the cost of goods sold is reduced and the profit is increased.

If sales are £50,000, an extra £1,000 profit is 2 per cent. If this makes the gross profit margin appear in the accounts as 20 per cent when the real figure is 18 per cent an owner who expected, say, 21 per cent, could then be misled. He might well accept a 1 per cent drop when he ought to be investigating one of 3 per cent.

Remember that 'purchases' and 'cost of goods sold' are not the same

As explained in Chapter 4 the purchase total is adjusted by opening and closing stocks so as to charge against sales the cost of goods *sold*.

Expenses

In the case of services bought in, such as electricity, telephone etc, it is often necessary to estimate the amount due for the period from the date to which the last invoice received was made up to the end of the accounting period.

Deposits received in advance

Some businesses take deposits or payments in advance from customers. Where money has been received in advance of the services being performed or the goods supplied, the amounts outstanding must be listed and carried forward as payments in advance from customers. Otherwise the profits will be inflated and too much tax may be payable, quite apart from the accounts failing to show a fair view of the position.

Thus the figures relating to the period covered by a profit and loss account are not necessarily just the cash you have paid or the invoices you have issued or received. Often these figures need adjusting to make them show the full story, not just those bits of it which happen to have been recorded so far.

The same principle applies for expenses. We must charge against profits the cost for the period, which is not necessarily what we have paid out.

How the arithmetic works for a small business which keeps records on a cash basis

If yours is a small business and you do not keep a full set of accounting records, this is how your accountant will work out your sales:

	£
Cash received during the period; say	10,000
Less accounts receivable at start of period	1,000
(ie debtors — amounts owing to you)	
	£9,000

If these debtors have been paid during the period, they will be included in the total of cash receipts above. Since they relate to sales in the previous period, we deduct them. If there are any still unpaid, they will be added back as part of the total still receivable at the end of the period: see below.

	£
Add accounts receivable at the end of the period (the reverse of the above)	800
Sales for period	£9,800

This example assumes that your invoicing is done promptly. However, if there were any goods delivered or, if you sell services, there were jobs completed by the end of the period which had not been invoiced, the value should be added in the total of accounts receivable so as to be part of the sales.

The purchases calculation is the same but uses the totals of money paid out and accounts payable (creditors — amounts owing by you) at the start and end of the period thus producing the figure of purchases of goods for resale received in the period.

To summarise the objective of the profit and loss account

The objective of the profit and loss account is to show the profits earned during the period from the sales made to customers and to charge the correct expenses both for goods 'used up' in supplies to customers and for services consumed in running the business during the period regardless of whether invoices have been raised or payments made. It is whether or not a liability has been incurred which decides whether a cost is a charge against the profit. The actual payment, in cash or by cheque, is merely the settlement of that liability.

Questions

☐ Return to the first page of this chapter and revise the question there.

Chapter 8

Points on the Accounts of a Public Company

Here are a few more points which may help you understand the accounts of large companies. This is not a treatise on public company accounts, but just the aspects which are most important for the layman and beginner to know about.

What do the published accounts of a company show?

As explained in Chapter 6, the Companies Acts do not require a detailed profit and loss account to be issued to shareholders or to be filed at Companies House. Your company's annual report may well be an expensive glossy production, but you will find that it does not show very much detailed information about sales and expenses when compared with internal management accounts. The latter contain confidential details which do not have to be made public.

Why are dividends paid to shareholders?

The ordinary shareholders take the biggest risk. They are the first to suffer if things go wrong and, should the company go out of business, they are the last to be paid after all the other creditors and lenders to the company. In return for their risk, they are entitled to all the surplus, should profits be made. In practice they cannot take all this out of the company both for tax reasons and because the business needs retained profit. Just as you expect interest on your savings in a building society or bank deposit account, the shareholder needs an income from his much higher risk investment. He does not always get it. He only receives dividends provided that there is enough *cash* to spare, not just profit. He is taxed on these dividends as unearned private income.

If the directors are also the shareholders, they may prefer to take their share of profits as salaries rather than as dividends. Sometimes a director, who is a major shareholder, waives his right to a dividend thus allowing other shareholders, who are not directors, to receive an income while leaving more cash in the company.

Is a dividend of £9,000 on share capital of £15,000 'big money'?

This is the figure from the example in Chapter 6. It is not what it seems. This comparison is with the nominal value of the shares which is the amount originally invested by the shareholders. This may have been many years ago in which case the profits retained in the company each year will have built up to substantial sums. These reserves are often as much as or even substantially greater than the nominal share capital.

The successful investment of these accumulated reserves will have increased the annual profit. The dividend will therefore have risen as well. If you re-calculate it as a percentage of the total shareholders' funds including reserves, you will find that it is much lower and that in many cases it represents no more than a modest return to the investor on his true investment. Here the shareholders' interest is £74,000 (see balance sheet).

In the case of a quoted company the Stock Exchange price for the shares may or may not be close to their value as shown by the balance sheet, depending upon the popularity or otherwise of the shares. The return to the investor is his dividend as a percentage of the price of his shares and it can be as low as 2 or 3 per cent even in a depressed share market. Only if there is serious doubt about the company's future profits will the dividend yield on the share price go much above 10 per cent. So high nominal dividends are not what they seem.

Dividend 'cover'

In some sets of accounts, the accumulated balance on the profit and loss account is added to the profit after tax before showing the dividends paid. This has the effect of hiding the key point of dividend 'cover', ie how much is paid out in dividends compared with the amount of profit retained.

In the example the cover is £19,000 (after the preference dividend) for £9,000 or about twice as much; see page 39.

Consolidated balance sheets

If a company has one or more subsidiaries (or 'associated' companies), they form a group of companies. None of the balance sheets of the individual companies will show the total value of the group. In the example previously explained, the holding company shows only the value of its investment in its subsidiaries or associates at cost. This may not reflect the real value, particularly if the

55

investment was made some years ago.

For this reason a consolidated balance sheet is prepared for a group of companies, which shows the overall position of the group. It adds together all the assets and liabilities of the individual companies as shown by their respective balance sheets.

Naturally the inter-company balances have to be cancelled against each other. This is simple since each amount is an asset in one balance sheet and a liability in the other.

The share capital of each subsidiary cancels against the investment in that subsidiary shown as a parent company asset. If the subsidiary is not fully owned, the consolidated balance sheet will show, as a liability, the minority interest representing the shares not owned. If the parent company paid more for its investment than the nominal value of the shares, the premium is shown as goodwill in the consolidated balance sheet.

This is a simplified explanation of how a consolidated balance sheet is prepared. To look at, it is much the same as an ordinary balance sheet, the main difference being that if any subsidiaries are not fully owned or if an associate company's figures are consolidated the value of the outsiders' share of the group assets will be shown under the heading 'minority interest'.

What matters to creditors or lenders?

Since the consolidated balance sheet shows the overall position it tends to be given prominence and the parent company's balance sheet is often ignored by readers of accounts. However, this can be a mistake if you are a creditor or are lending money either to the parent company or to one of its subsidiaries.

The group, as consolidated, has no legal existence. It is individual companies whom one must sue in any dispute and, unless guarantees have been given, they are not responsible for each other's debts. It is usually impossible, legally speaking, to force a parent company to make good a deficiency in the assets of one of its subsidiaries.

It might be possible to realise the assets of a wholly owned subsidiary if you could force the parent into liquidation but it could be a long business if the subsidiary's directors were independent and reluctant to cooperate.

Remember that 51 per cent of a company is not enough to force a liquidation against the wishes of the other shareholders. Many consolidated balance sheets also include the assets of associate companies of which less than half the shares are owned. The creditors of the holding company are probably powerless to realise the assets of an associate company. Almost certainly their only possible course is to sell the shares and it might be very difficult to find a buyer for these unless they are quoted on the Stock Exchange.

So while consolidated balance sheets give vital information about the overall picture, they can be very misleading if used to assess the security for a loan or an ordinary trading debt.

Look also at the parent company's figures (the holding company's balance sheet is published as well as the consolidated figures) or at those of the particular subsidiary with which you deal. Enquire for a parent company guarantee if in doubt.

What about income from associated companies?

If company A owns less than 50 per cent of company B, B is not a subsidiary but is often treated in the balance sheet of company A as an associated company, as explained in the previous section.

The significance of the 'associated company' heading is that the share of B's profits, which relates to the shares in it which A owns, is then brought in to A's consolidated accounts. This is in contrast to treating the income as being merely the actual dividend received.

One result of this is to show the group income as much larger than the amount over which the parent company's directors have direct control. They may not be able to force payment of a larger share of their associated company's profits and their own reported income may overstate the security available to a lender or creditor.

There is often a big difference between the dividend paid and the total profit applicable to a shareholding. This will depend upon the policy of the paying company, how much it needs to retain to pay for expansion plans, and so on.

There have been many cases of companies holding valuable investments in other companies which were shown at a fraction of their true value, both because this was stated at a historic cost often many years old, and because the income shown ignored the profits retained by the paying company. Often it was very difficult for outsiders to appreciate the facts for lack of detailed information. On the Stock Exchange this led to some unsatisfactory situations in which companies were taken over for prices vastly greater than their shares had been valued at on the basis of the published information available immediately before the take-over bid. The associated company method of accounting was therefore adopted in order to reflect the true position more closely.

Net assets per share

This is a figure often quoted in the financial press in connection with public companies. In the example, the calculation is:

	£
Shareholders' interest	74,000
Less preference shares	10,000
	£64,000
Divide by 15,000 = per share	£4.27

Questions

Check your answers with the text.

- ☐ What is the difference between a shareholder and a director?
- ☐ Why do shareholders need dividends?
- ☐ What is dividend cover?
- ☐ What is the difference between the balance sheet of a parent company and that of the whole group (ie the consolidated balance sheet)?

Chapter 9

What the Profit and Loss Account Tells You

Individual figures in your accounts mean little. It is in comparison with other figures that the key facts emerge.

Assessing your profits

Your profit and loss account shows you the result of your trading. Is it satisfactory?

Sales — did you sell more?

How much was the sales increase last year? Did it keep pace with inflation in the price of the goods or services you sell or did a rise in *money* totals, resulting from higher prices, conceal a fall in the *volume* of business?

Sales — how much could you have sold?

Is there a limit to your possible sales and if so, how close did you get? If you are providing a service, you are really selling time. There may be skills and/or materials involved as well but it is time you are selling and there is only so much of it, unless you take on more staff. Once a service has sold enough hours to cover its fixed costs, every extra hour sold is profit subject only to materials and any other direct expenses. So a key factor in the profitability of a service is how close it gets to selling all its available time. On the other hand, once it is near to its maximum potential, it may only be able to increase sales by raising prices or taking on staff, which will increase costs — possibly more than sales.

Even a business selling goods may have an effective limit to its market. A shop on a housing estate normally can only hope to sell to people living on the estate. Their expenditure on any particular line of goods will be limited and the shop cannot hope for business beyond that limit.

These are simple examples but no business sells in a vacuum. What are the constraints on yours? How close are you to the effective limits to your volume of sales?

Are you making the right gross profit?

In Chapter 7 on the profit and loss account, I mentioned gross profit. Of all the key figures, this is the least understood, so here is some more on this important subject.

This is what gross profit means

Suppose you are a shopkeeper selling cakes at £2 each, which you buy at £1.50. You make a profit of 50p which is 25 per cent of the selling price. For simplicity, let's assume you sell only cakes.

If you dispose of 200 cakes a week, your gross profit is 25 per cent on sales of 200 × £2 = £400, ie £100 or 50p per cake. If the fixed costs of running your shop are £90 per week, you have a net profit of £10, or 5p per cake.

What happens to net profit if you raise your sales to 300 cakes per week? Stop here for a moment and work out for yourself, before reading on, how much your gross profit is and the net profit per cake.

300 cakes = sales £600 at 25 per cent = gross profit £150 (50p per cake) less fixed costs £90 = net profit £60 or 20p per cake. Your sales are up by half, gross profit has remained unchanged but net profit per cake has multiplied *four* times from 5p to 20p and the amount of net profit *six* times from £10 to £100!

The reason, of course, is that the fixed costs (wages, rent, rates, electricity, etc) remain the same whether you sell one cake or 300. Perhaps a higher volume of sales creates a few more telephone calls or a little more wear and tear on fittings and equipment but such extra costs are insigificant. Of course, wages will rise when your existing staff can no longer cope but this will be a major jump due to extra staff being taken on and will relate directly to the number of people you employ, not to the volume of sales as such, even though the latter is the cause.

Once you have paid your fixed costs, each extra cake sold produces 50p more net profit and that net profit spread over all the cakes sold rises dramatically until you have to engage extra staff.

Some cakes are wasted

Sadly, life is not so simple that that is the end of the story. Not every cake you buy gets sold. Here is why:

☐ Some get pushed to the back during busy sales periods and fresh stock goes in front by mistake, so the others go past their 'sell by' dates and have to be eaten by the owner or given to the staff.

☐ A few just fail to sell — the fillings, sizes, etc — are not quite what customers want that week.

☐ Other cakes are spoilt in the window when the sun comes out unexpectedly and staff are too busy to erect the blind.

☐ Occasionally you guess the demand completely wrong: perhaps the weather alters unexpectedly, there is a local scare about hygiene, another shop is prosecuted for selling cream cakes which are not fresh. Whatever the reason, it temporarily cuts sales and you find you have overbought.

☐ You deliver a large order to a local caterer and include an extra cake in error, or you price your invoice to him incorrectly, or you calculate the total wrongly.

☐ Your supplier short delivers you and you fail to check in time. Alternatively, he overcharges you per cake or makes a calculating error in his invoice which you do not spot. Occasionally he delivers the wrong cakes, too many cakes or substandard cakes and you do not discover these errors in time to claim credit. Some such mistakes by suppliers are genuine errors; others are deliberate fraud, often by staff of the supplier rather than the owner, as in the next example.

☐ You are busy when your supplier delivers and you do not notice the van driver removing one of the cartons which you have just hurriedly signed for. He sells it for cash elsewhere.

☐ One of your sales girls give special prices to her friends without your knowledge or permission. A second assistant gets into financial trouble and starts to 'borrow' from the till. Another assistant has a sweet tooth and either eats on the premises or takes home cakes which are still fresh and in date. Customers pilfer a proportion of your stock.

☐ Your store room is crowded and you trip over a carton squashing it and sending another flying, rendering cakes in both cartons unsaleable.

☐ Your competitor down the road finds a new source of cheaper supplies and he cuts prices, forcing you to follow suit.

☐ Some of your cakes sell by weight and there are minor but consistent undercharges to customers. Others are priced too low by mistake.

I hope your shop is not subject to such a catalogue of calamities all at once but there is no business which is free from all of them. Everyone has wastage of one kind or another. Whatever your trade or industry, you're bound to have similar problems.

The results of poor control of gross profit
Suppose that all the losses add up to just 1 per cent of the cakes you sell, ie three cakes on 300, value £6 at sale prices. Your figures are then:

	£
Sales: 297 at £2	594
Cost of goods sold: 300 at £1.50	450
(because you have to write off the missing 6 as well as the 294 sold)	
Gross profit	144
Net profit	54

ie a reduction of 10 per cent from the previous profit of £60.

This level of loss may not seem too bad, but what if the losses are 3 per cent — nine cakes = £18 sales? The net profit is then down from £60 to £42, a fall of 30 per cent. That is quite a cut in your personal pay packet! And the dreadful reality is that 3 per cent of sales is on the low side for many businesses for pilferage losses, let alone all the others. Since many make less than 10 per cent of sales as net profit, you can see how serious this is.

Your gross profit is vital!
In the example of a profit and loss account in Chapter 4, gross profit (GP) has fallen from 24½ to 23 per cent. 1½ per cent on sales of £249,560 is £3,743. On the net profit of £10,000 this is 37.4 per cent. But one ought to compare it with the 'super' profit of £800 on which it is 468 per cent! In fact this loss of GP is the main reason why the super profit has fallen and is so small in relation to the size of the business.

Small variations in GP often have a major impact upon the real profitability of the business. Usually it is easier to save 1 per cent of GP on sales than it is 10 per cent of an expense item. In the example given 1 per cent on sales is £2,496 which dwarfs the likely savings resulting from a blitz on expenses.

In retailing, similar shops start with roughly the same gross profit to play with. One supermarket's margins will be similar to another's; a small grocer buys on similar terms to other small grocers. As fixed expenses for equivalent shops are also similar, the main reason for the big differences in the net profit earned by comparable businesses is control of gross profit.

In non-retail businesses, other factors may play a bigger part but it is *always* true that the most effective way to raise profits is to tackle gross profit, because this is the largest figure which is susceptible to profit improvement.

Boosting sales is *not* an alternative; it could even make things worse by concentrating your attention on the wrong problems. Higher sales at lower prices do not necessarily mean more gross profit. Improving your cost of sales by better purchasing or more efficient use of materials or labour could be a more effective way of raising gross profit.

Let's look at it yet another way: to illustrate the arithmetic of wastage, consider what happens if you mark up the theoretical cost of your products by 33⅓ per cent. By theoretical cost, I mean what it should cost you to make an item, given normal usage of materials. A mark-up cost of 33⅓ per cent is the same as a margin on sales of 25 per cent. Thus £100 at cost becomes £133.33 of sales.

Suppose, however, that you have a wastage of materials in production of 5 per cent above the norm and loss of finished product due to unsaleable goods or to pilferage, also of 5 per cent. Your cost becomes £105 instead of £100 while the sales proceeds fall from £133.33 to £126.67. Your gross profit is thus only £21.67 instead of £33.33. Instead of a gross margin of 25 per cent (£33.33 on £133.33), you earn 17.1 per cent (£21.67 on £126.67). Frightening, isn't it? That might be the whole of your net profit gone to waste. Thus:

	Theoretical figures £		Actual figures £
Sales	400,000	down 5%	380,000
Cost of sales	300,000	up 5%	315,000
Gross profit 25%	100,000	17.1%	65,000
Overheads	65,000		65,000
Net profit 8.75%	£35,000		£Nil

The business should be profitable. Instead it makes no money. Since waste goes with inefficiency generally, including in the book-keeping, the chances are that the owner's records aren't good enough to show the cause of the loss and that he has no idea where they are happening.

Whether or not my figures are typical in your case is not the point. Whatever your own situation, you will find that the potential impact of wastage on your gross profit dwarfs in importance every other daily consideration affecting the management of your money.

I'm not merely pontificating on the subject from the safety of a desk. I too have problems in minimising wastage of what I sell — my time. They are just different ones from those of a business handling goods. My message is that your gross profit margin deserves your best attention.

If you don't earn it gross, you can't have it net!

Factors which affect gross profit

Here are some of the key factors which affect how much gross profit you earn:

1. Wastage of all kinds: many of the causes have already been mentioned.
2. Pricing policy — low price/high volume or high price/low volume and discounts offered.
3. Skill in buying the right goods at the right price and in the right quantities.
4. Cash discounts obtained for prompt payment.
5. Manufacturing efficiency (if applicable), ie:
   (a) effective use of materials
   (b) minimal machine downtime
   (c) best use of production labour/efficient scheduling
   (d) quality control.
6. Time charge-out ratios (for service industries and the professions)
   (a) ratio of hours charged out to those available from owners and staff
   (b) control of work on own administration
   (c) control of sickness/absenteeism etc.

There are three important figures in your accounts, errors in which affect the gross profit.

1. *The stock valuation.* Obviously, if you have not counted and valued your stock accurately at the prices you paid, your gross profit will be distorted.
2. *Outstanding bills.* Your purchases figure, which is part of the cost of sales calculation, cannot be correct if you have not

64

included all the invoices outstanding for goods you have used or counted in stock. See Chapter 7 if you are unclear about this.

3. *Sales on credit.* All deliveries to customers made prior to stock-taking must be invoiced if the sales figure is to be correct.

Analyse your gross profit

If your business sells different goods at widely differing profit margins, it pays to analyse your gross profit because an average will be meaningless. For example, a public house may have the following sales:

	Gross profit %	Sales £	Gross profit £
Bar	35	100,000	35,000
Wines	60	30,000	18,000
Food	60	80,000	48,000
Accommodation	N/A	50,000	50,000
	Average 58.1	260,000	151,000

The *average* gross profit percentage, 58.1 per cent, is useless as a ratio for judging the results of the pub. It is made up of margins which vary widely and it is merely a statistic resulting from that particular sales mix. In order to assess the figures, it is necessary to look at them broken down by section of the business.

To illustrate this, suppose that the barman stole £200 per week, (£10,000 pa). In analysed accounts this would show up as a hole in the bar gross profit which would drop to only 27.8 per cent, ie £25,000 on £90,000. It would be evident that something was wrong.

If the figure were not analysed, the theft would reduce the overall gross profit to 56.4 per cent, ie £141,000 on £250,000. How could one spot the problem? Most likely it would go undetected because there would be no easy way of calculating what the gross profit ought to be.

So if your gross profits on different items vary widely, make sure you split your sales somehow. Even if you have to estimate the split using purchases grossed up by assumed profit margins, this is better than nothing.

Wages and salaries

Staff costs are always important though more so in some businesses than in others. In service industries, repair workshops and catering, for example, they tend to be vital because sales often depend upon the efficiency of the people who provide the service. Thus a café at peak periods can only improve its sales if customers are served more quickly.

Where labour itself is being sold, as in a repair workshop, the number of hours charged to customers, as a percentage of those paid for to staff, is a key ratio. Overtime hours worked may well be another.

After cost of sales, staff costs in most businesses are the largest expense and therefore offer the most scope for economy. It is good practice to put them at the top of the expenses list for this reason. Many sets of accounts hide the facts on staff costs by splitting them up under different headings; such analysis is often meaningless and merely conceals the size of this important figure.

Put all the elements which make up your staff costs together. Pension contributions, travel costs and car expenses are examples of items which are just as much a cost of employing people as their actual wages. They are usually shown as separate totals but should be listed together, not scattered haphazardly.

Other expenses

In some businesses, advertising and sales promotion costs such as catalogues, brochures, etc are major items and need careful control in consequence.

The rest of your expenses are unlikely to matter very much. You need to know what they are and to keep track of how the totals are working out but some, such as rent and rates, can only be altered by moving premises. Few, if any, will be big enough to matter as much as gross profit and wages.

The telephone is one cost which does have to be watched more carefully; yet unless you have one of the sophisticated machines which record each call, it is difficult to keep any control on it at all.

Here's a tip which at least will help you to see what is happening. Your telephone bill is made up of three elements: a standing charge, the number of units used and the price per unit. Keep a special record of your bills showing each of these elements plus the total of the bill. Then you will be able to see whether the key one, the number of units, is going up. Higher bills could be due to changes in the standing charges or the price per unit. It's the usage you need to check on and a record kept over a couple of years is very helpful in showing the pattern of what is happening.

Concentrate on your key figures

In most businesses there are only two or three figures which have a major impact on profits and which also change daily or weekly. They are usually sales, gross profit margins, wages (or staff use) and perhaps one other, depending on the business. These four items have a far greater impact than all the other details put together.

Go through your detailed costs once or twice a year to see if you can cut out items, stop using this or that service, simplify equipment such as telephones, improve heating efficiency etc. Then leave them alone and concentrate on the things you can change day by day, where improvements can yield really big benefits.

Figures as a percentage of sales

Since only the gross profit varies directly with sales, this is the most useful profit and loss ratio.

Staff costs as a percentage of annual sales over a period of years may be significant because it can reveal trends. To control staff costs, however, one must refer to numbers employed, pay rises negotiated etc.

In some cases advertising and promotion are a big cost which requires highlighting as a percentage of sales, because average industry ratios are a useful comparison with the competition.

Most of the other expenses of a business are either not big enough in relation to GP and wages to matter, or are fixed. Other expense percentages, therefore, are not usually key ratios and it is pointless to calculate them.

Net profit percentage on sales

This is a useful guide to progress of a business over a period of years. Sometimes it is a valid comparison between businesses in the same trade. However, its value is as a relative figure in comparison with others. Absolute percentage profits on sales vary enormously. Even in the same trade, different businesses may have quite different methods of operation. One may process customers' materials while another supplies its own. The sales totals will be very different to achieve the same net profit.

Net profit expressed as return on net capital employed is a key ratio which is dealt with under balance sheet key ratios.

Do not misuse ratios

In the example of the net profits per cake quoted earlier, the rise from 5p to 20p per cake was interesting, exciting, big news. But what did it actually tell you about the business other than that profits were improving fast? Nothing, because the ratio, as a basis for management action, is meaningless and is of interest only as an annual trend indicator. Many people who ought to know better waste their own and others' time on ratios which are either meaningless or misleading in terms of day-to-day management.

Some managers (some accountants too) regard ratios as an end in themselves, regardless of what useful action may result. They insist on calculating them and they use the figures which are readily available, whether or not these are comparable or relevant, and without troubling to ask themselves why. The effect on the morale of their subordinates or colleagues, who know the results to be useless but who are expected to respond to or explain them, can be disastrous. Might you be guilty?

Questions

Check your answers with the text.

- ☐ Which are the key ratios in the example given and discussed above?
- ☐ Which are the key ratios in your own business?
- ☐ Why are they relevant and why do they matter?

Chapter 10

What the Balance Sheet Tells You

As with the profit and loss account, the balance sheet will only tell you the right story if you understand how the figures relate to each other. Ratios are often more revealing than the figures on which they are based.

This chapter explains various terms which need to be understood because there are no simple substitutes for them. Besides, if you want the best out of your accountant, it helps to be able to talk his language.

Are the figures typical?

The balance sheet only gives figures at one date. This may or may not be typical — many financial year ends are at quiet periods to ease stock-taking, etc.

When considering balance sheet ratios, therefore:

1. Consider whether the figures used reflect the normal position.
2. Use the correct figures which relate to each other; thus debtor balances relate to sales immediately prior to the balance sheet date, not to the average for the whole period. Also they include value added tax (VAT), unlike the sales figure, so to compare the two, one must add the VAT on to the sales total, if it applies.

Note: The figures in this chapter use the balance sheet in Chapter 5.

Capital employed

The total funds in use by the business, ie the total of its assets. In the example this is £70,900.

Net capital employed

Total assets less current liabilities, except the bank overdraft. Current liabilities, principally creditors, are in effect finance provided by outsiders for short periods. Thus the net capital which the owner has to provide is reduced by the normal trade credit he receives. The overdraft, in contrast, is a method of financing part of his cash needs and does not arise automatically from trading. Therefore it should not reduce the net capital employed figure which in the example is £70,900 – £11,000 = £59,900.

An important measure of the profitability of the business is the return earned upon net capital employed; see page 73.

Working capital

The cash required to operate the business from day to day, ie to pay for stocks, debtors, advance payments to creditors, deposits etc. The amount is reduced by creditors, advance payments from customers etc. Thus current assets less current liabilities represents at the date of the balance sheet the working capital in use by the business. Any bank overdraft should be added back to the net balance for the reason explained above under net capital employed. It is more realistic to regard it as a means of funding than as part of working capital.

Net capital employed and working capital

The respective figures from the example are set out to show how the two terms differ.

	Net capital employed £	Working capital £
Fixed assets and goodwill	29,400	N/A
Current assets	41,500	41,500
	70,900	41,500
Less current liabilities except bank overdraft	11,000	11,000
Net capital employed/working capital	59,900	30,500
Funded by:		
the bank	18,000	18,000
the owner	31,900	12,500
long-term loan	10,000	N/A
	£59,900	£30,500

In this case the bank is providing 59 per cent of the net working capital, which is all right but the bank might not wish the proportion to go higher. See also under balance sheet ratios.

Too high a proportion of bank finance is often a sign of

overtrading. This occurs when sales expand beyond the capacity of the business to provide the necessary working capital for stock and debtors — hence increased borrowings.

Current assets to current liabilities

This is an important test. The right ratio varies from trade to trade and with the nature of the assets. In retailing one might be happy with anything over 1.25:1 because stocks, correctly managed, are fairly easily cleared and are often largely funded by creditors.

In manufacturing stocks have to be held longer and in various stages of production so that one cannot rely as much upon credit. A ratio of at least 1.5:1 is desirable.

In the example it is £41,500 to £29,000 or 1.4 (last year 1.3).

Another factor in judging a particular situation is the extent to which the bank is financing current assets. An overdraft, being repayable upon demand, is not the same as normal trade credit, which will continue so long as the trade reputation of the business is good.

Properly managed businesses keep their current ratios in line. A ratio which is below average for the particular trade is a sign of one or more faults:

(a) losses eroding cash.
(b) bad cash planning — using short-term money to pay for fixed assets or to fund long-term projects.

While an above average current ratio may reflect financial strength, it may also suggest idle cash and a business which is not fully exploiting its resources.

Liquidity — the acid test

This is a more severe test of the ability of the business to pay its debts, sometimes called the 'acid test'. It is the ratio of quick assets — those current assets which can quickly be turned into cash — to current liabilities.

In the example, debtors of £6,000 compare with current liabilities of £29,000. Stocks do not count as quick assets because, in most cases, only a part of them could be realised quickly. Often that part of stocks which is saleable at once is matched by debtors from whom rapid payment is not obtainable.

The seriousness of the position in the example depends upon when the tax is payable and upon the attitude of the bank. Should it put on pressure for a reduction in the overdraft this could only come from cutting stocks.

In the example, the business has an overdraft. Naturally, if there is cash in the bank, this counts as part of quick assets.

Debtors to sales: expressed in number of days' sales

This is debtors including VAT compared with sales after adding back VAT. The correct ratio is that of debtors to sales for the weeks immediately prior to the date of the balance sheet, *not* debtors to the average of the annual sales. Naturally, where sales fluctuate in the course of a year, more detail is required than is shown in the profit and loss account.

In the example little credit is given and debtors are just over a week's sales, assuming VAT at 15 per cent.

The ratio indicates whether a proper credit control policy is in force. The correct number of days outstanding varies of course according to the credit terms you offer your customers.

Stocks to usage (cost of sales): expressed in number of days' usage held

Again the stocks at the balance sheet date are often low in comparison with the average so that the ratio requires enquiry before acceptance as valid. Also not all stocks shown necessarily relate to cost of sales. Some may be stationery, fuel or other expense items.

In the example, trade stocks of £34,200 against usage (cost of sales) of £192,160 or £3,695 weekly suggests 9¼ weeks' usage held (last year £3,210 pw = 8.4 weeks). This might be reasonable for a manufacturer or retailer working on high profit margins, but would be too high for a grocer, for example, whose stocks should be fast moving because they are perishable and on low margins. But is the June stock figure representative?

In the case of a manufacturer, cost of sales might include some labour and other production costs: so might the stock valuation so check before accepting the ratio. Labour and other costs must be in both the figures used in calculating the ratio or not at all.

The stocks ratio indicates the effectiveness of the control of buying, skill in forecasting sales, the efficiency of the stockroom and, where applicable, the efficiency in production. It is vitally important. Bad stock control ties up both cash and space. It causes stock losses through damage, excess quantities, etc, and makes it more difficult to bring in new lines, change policy to meet new conditions, etc.

Creditors to purchases and expenses: expressed in number of days' purchases

Recent purchases may not be typical. As an example, a build-up of stocks for Christmas might invalidate a ratio of average purchases during the year to creditors at 30 November. To see the true picture you would need the purchases for the weeks prior to that date, not the annual average.

Remember that creditors include VAT but purchases do not.

In the example, purchases are £199,360 and expenses about £19,000, ignoring wages and rent which are not incurred on credit. Adding VAT at 15 per cent, the total is £251,000, or about £4,800 weekly average. Less than two weeks' credit suggests a failure to use normal trade terms. If prompt payment is being made to obtain cash discounts, why has the gross profit ratio fallen? Or is the June creditors total not representative?

The ratio indicates the extent to which creditors are paid promptly. This has various implications concerning reputation, discounts obtained, etc.

Net profits to net capital employed

In the example, net capital employed is £70,900 − £11,000 = £59,900. Adding back interest on the overdraft and loan of £3,500 gives a profit of £13,500 or 22.5 per cent (last year £12,600 on £56,400 = 22.3 per cent). This is well ahead of the interest cost on the money borrowed.

Super profit to proprietor's interest

But look at this ratio: super profit of £800 on the owner's interest of £31,900 is about 2.5 per cent. If the calculation is adjusted for interest and loans the figures are £4,300 on £59,900 = 7.2 per cent (last year £4,300 on £56,400 = 7.6 per cent). In recent years one has often been able to earn as much or more simply by leaving one's money in a bank!

The calculation of true profit, ie after charging a working wage for the owner as a percentage of his interest in the business, is often a salutary exercise.

You must aim to earn a premium over the return obtainable from selling the business, taking a job and investing the cash. Otherwise why bother with the extra effort and responsibility and the longer working hours?

Equally, if expansion is planned, the cash borrowed, or realised from investments, to pay for it must earn a profit in excess of its interest cost.

Suppose your current super profit on net capital employed is 17.5 per cent on £12,600. This should not necessarily rule out borrowing money at, say, 20 per cent. If, for example, £3,000 could be borrowed at 20 per cent for a project which would generate extra sales of £10,000 at gross profit of 23 per cent without extra staff or other significant expenses, the result would be as follows:

	Super profit before interest £	Net capital employed £	Percentage return %
Current	2,200	12,600	17.5
New sales £10,000 at 23%			
GP = extra profit	2,300		
Cash borrowed at 20%			
interest cost	(600)	3,000	
New result	£3,900	£15,600	25.0

While this example may be a little optimistic in propounding a sales increase of £10,000 without increasing overheads, it does illustrate how figures need to be seen in perspective, not in isolation.

In this example, the current figures might reflect under-use of assets and staff which is remedied by the new project even though the money costs 20 per cent. Hence all the extra gross profit comes through as net profit.

Questions

Check your answers with the text.

- ☐ What is:
  - — capital employed?
  - — net capital employed?
  - — working capital?
- ☐ What are the seven ratios mentioned above?
- ☐ In what form is each expressed?

Chapter 11

How Cash Circulates in a Business

Why do cash ratios matter?

Many of the key business ratios previously explained reveal the efficiency with which cash is used. A business can get away with bad cash use reflected in poor liquidity, high debtors, stocks and creditors, heavy overdrafts etc provided its profitability is high. But as soon as anything goes wrong, its cash shortage puts it at risk. Any loss of confidence by its creditors squeezes it hard. A business which is basically profitable but which mismanages its cash can easily be toppled by a temporary setback into liquidation because it has no room to manoeuvre.

A basic rule of cash management

Fixed assets and long-term development should be financed by retained profits or by loans on fixed repayment terms. That way one can plan for repayment of the cash out of profits.

Bank overdrafts are only suitable for financing current assets such as debtors and stock. Being repayable on demand, they should only be invested in assets which can be realised quickly. Otherwise you are in the dangerous position of investing long and borrowing short.

Cash is your lifeblood!

Businesses go bust for lack of cash, not necessarily because they are not making profits. What actually breaks them is inability to pay their bills.

The water tank chart

How well does your business use its money? Efficient cash control is vital to stability and profits. Perhaps you realise that your equipment, stocks and amounts owed by customers are 'money' to be controlled, just like your bank balance, but do your colleagues or your employees?

An understanding of how cash circulates in a business is

important not only for the boss but for the staff too. Even in the smaller business, the boss needs the cooperation of employees if the amount of cash tied up is to be minimised. My tank chart is especially valuable in getting the idea across to non-accountants because it explains it in physical terms.

The chart shows, in engineers' language, how a business uses money. Cash circulates like water which flows through a system of tanks, partly by gravity and partly through a pump.

Where does the money come from?

At the start of the business the owner(s) provide loans or pay up share capital, the bank may make a loan or provide an overdraft facility. This finance flows into the bank account and it's all the money there is. It can't come from anywhere else.

Gravity feed

It's easy to spend money. From the bank account cash flows out at the turn of a tap, so to speak, into fixed assets and stocks. Some is lost as stock wastage. A little comes back when assets are sold off.

In some businesses, there ought to be an extra tank for research and development costs carried forward in the balance sheet because they relate to new products not yet launched. It's all too easy to sink cash into R and D.

Perhaps less readily, cash is then absorbed in giving credit for sales. Some leaks away as bad debts. How much each tank absorbs depends on how you run your business.

The gross profit margin

The cost in cash of a sale is what you have spent in producing the item or providing the service. To that cost is added your profit margin to make the amount owing to the customer which is shown in your balance sheet. This profit inflates the debtors' tank, but is not yet cash in hand.

The pump house gets the money back in

From then on cash only flows back up round the system when pumped via the financial control pump house which is powered by budgets, cash flow forecasts, stock control etc.

How cash circulates in a business

Money in from debtors

This is a temporary holding tank included to emphasise how sales are only cash once debts are collected. From this tank payments are made for cash expenses and the other tanks are refilled.

Trade credit tank

If you pay your suppliers regularly, the trade credit tank will continue its gravity feed which finances stocks. But should an interruption in supply from 'Money in from debtors' occur, it will quickly run dry as creditors withdraw facilities.

Bank account

Finally, the bank account tank is replenished. This has three sources of supply:

1. retained profit
2. owner's capital (in shares or loans)
3. bank overdraft or other loans.

Both the owner's and the bank's tanks need periodic replenishment if they are to be able and willing to continue providing the extra finance which is needed as inflation raises stock values etc, let alone to pay for expansion.

Too much cash in one tank reduces the cash available elsewhere

Since the cash supply in the business is limited an excess in one tank must drain off from another, perhaps causing a shortage. The excess may be caused by poor control of spending decisions or by failure to collect debts. This reflects itself in the various ratios previously discussed.

What are the financial decisions made in your organisation? Who takes them?

These are catch questions to see whether the previous message has sunk in! Before continuing, consider how the money is spent in your business and who takes the decisions. Refer back to the water tank chart when working out your answers and write them down here under the headings:

Decisions to spend.
Who takes them?

The decisions are made thus

The decision to spend is irrevocable once the order is placed for an asset, such as a piece of equipment, a vehicle etc, or for goods or materials for resale or use in manufacture. Once a sale is made on credit to a customer, cash has been committed to that deal.

These are the points at which the commitment is made. The subsequent payment is inevitable sooner or later. Cash management must therefore start with control over the placing of orders. The management of the accounts payable (creditors) ledger, or invoices outstanding, can be helpful, particularly in squeezing a little extra credit when money is particularly tight, but it is really only tinkering with the problem. Once the order is placed it is usually too late to avert the need to make the payment.

The third decision point listed, that of granting credit to customers, is not the same as the others. No actual payment is made; on the contrary, money is subsequently received from the customer. Nevertheless, there is a cost of granting credit. This is not just the interest charges on the money which is outstanding. Every time goods go out of the business on credit, they have to be replaced by other goods in order to maintain stocks. Frequently it is not the production manager or the buyer who causes an order for goods or materials in the first place, but the sales manager who creates the need to buy in further supplies by making the credit sale in the first place.

Whether these jobs are all done by one man or by a team of people, it is important to understand how the different decisions interlock with each other.

I don't want to overstress the spending of money by the sales manager when he grants credit. His job, after all, is to obtain sales. However, he should understand that the responsibility for operating the company's credit policy starts with him and that this is not just red tape for the benefit of the accounts department.

The arithmetic of credit control

Do you understand the arithmetic involved in a bad debt? If your gross profit is 30 per cent you have materials and direct expenses in a £100 bad debt value £70. To recover that loss of £70, you will therefore need to make a further £230 of sales. This is bad enough, but consider the situation if you take the net profit on the sale. Since the collection of the money from the customer is the last operation in the whole chain of events, it is reasonable to charge to a sale more than just the direct cost of producing the goods or the services. After paying all the overheads, salaries etc of the business, many net profits are no more than 10 per cent or less of the sales value. To recover the real loss on a bad debt of £100 at a net profit margin of 10 per cent, ie £90, you will need to make no less than £900 of new sales.

Even if you argue that this overstates the case because the administrative and other overhead costs will not increase in proportion to the extra sales required to recover the bad debt, the true increase in sales needed to cover the bad debt must surely lie at least halfway between the two figures, ie around £500 to £600.

The executive team

I hope that I have now persuaded you that the financial decisions in your business are not taken by just one person. It is the entire executive team which is involved.

Even in the smallest organisations this is true. The small shopkeeper does not have executives as such, but his staff are, or should be, involved in taking stock and keeping track of goods required etc. However small you are, if you have not managed to involve your staff so that they understand the importance of minimising stocks, having the right goods to hand to meet customers' requirements etc and they take an active part in helping you to achieve those objectives, you are not running your business at its maximum effectiveness.

In the larger organisation, the team may consist of one or more of the following executive staff:

Buyer
Production manager
Development manager
Research manager
Despatch manager
Head storeman
Sales manager
and, of course, the Boss.

Why the research manager?

This applies only to those readers whose businesses spend a significant sum of money each year on research and development (R and D) of one kind or another. These businesses should have a subheading or division of the fixed assets tank in the water tank chart between fixed assets and research and development.

Research and development is a tank of enormous size into which huge sums can flow with no resulting value whatever.

The problem of R and D is always to make it start producing cash. This is not a matter of 'as quickly as possible', so much as 'within reasonable time'. The scientist or technician always wants to perfect his product before putting it on the market. This is in direct conflict with the need of the organisation, which is to get some cash coming in to offset the continuing expenditure.

If R and D produces a product, which generates cash to pay for the continuing cost of improving it, it is very valuable to the company. On the other hand, R and D which simply absorbs cash over an indefinite period in indefinite amounts may very well destroy it. However good the potential, however technically exciting the project, future possibilities never paid current bills.

Are your priorities muddled?

Cash is 'spent' by the people who order things or who grant credit to customers, not when cheques are signed. Often orders, particularly for stock items, are initiated by junior staff who are ignorant of policy decisions on product development, discontinuing of lines etc. Resulting mistakes can tie up money in surplus or unusable stocks.

Say a clerk orders 10,000 units of a component for a product of which you have been selling 2000 a month but which is due to be phased out shortly. The financial loss will not only be the useless stock which no one wants, even for scrap; by the time the problem is identified, the components will have taken up expensive space in your stockroom, got in the way of the efficient running of your stores and occupied people's time to check them in etc. The consequent inefficiency may have cost as much as the direct loss.

Orders for stock from suppliers merit the attention of senior management. Yet they rarely get it. It is often not them but the purchase of a typewriter which requires the approval of the managing director. The potential loss is very small; his secretary understands typewriters better and, even if she got it wrong, the machine could be sold quickly at a limited loss. How many muddled priorities like this are there in your organisation?

What about your own priorities?

If, as the boss or the financial director, you spend your time pushing paper on relatively trivial matters because they are easy to pin down instead of on those aspects of the business of fundamental importance financially, you can hardly expect your staff or your colleagues not to copy you.

You must delegate effectively. That means getting your staff to take responsibility for detail and, if you employ managers, they too must delegate in the same way. People down the line of authority won't handle responsibility well, however, unless they understand why. Hence the importance of using the tank chart to explain why the details matter: details like those computer statements we all get, which are obviously wrong and which provide the perfect excuse not to pay. The 'system' just sends them out, when a casual check by staff would pick up the errors.

Details like that despatch note not yet passed for invoicing, which represents money owed by a customer who won't pay until he gets his bill: or the pile of goods, stuck in the wrong place and hidden behind other stock, which is urgently needed on the production line and represents cash which the business can't ask for until the order goes out. Explaining could make all the difference to the way they take responsibility for the detail in your organisation.

To summarise

Cash disappears easily into fixed assets, stocks and debtors. It only comes back when customers pay. To make sure they pay and to keep to a minimum the money you need to run the business, you must exercise financial control.

Cash is scarce. Conserving it should be the concern of everyone who works in the business. That means telling people why it matters and how they can help. The tank chart is a good way of doing this because it sets the matter out in a way which people find easy to understand. Are you sure *you* understand? Try filling in the blank chart now.

How cash circulates in a business

Exercise: Fill in descriptions in the correct places. They are listed at the bottom of the chart.

Debtors	Bank: Overdraft facility	Stock wastage
Trade creditors	Actual account	Pump house
Fixed assets	Bad debts	Owner and lenders
Stocks	Wages and other cash	Gross profit margin
	expenses	
	Money in from debtors	

Chapter 12

What the Statement of Source and Application of Cash Tells You

In Chapter 11, we saw how cash circulates in a business. Chapter 1 pointed out that the inability to pay its bills puts a business out of business and that controlling your cash is just as important as making a profit. Now I'll explain what I call the statement of source and application of cash.

Up to now, I have said that a set of accounts consists only of the profit and loss account and the balance sheet. These are indeed the two main documents but, although they show whether or not a profit has been earned and what the state of the business is at the end of its financial year, they do not show clearly what has happened to the cash. They do not explain how the profit relates to the bank balance.

Since it is possible to earn a good profit and yet find oneself even deeper into the red, this is important. It is the statement of source and application of cash which forms the missing link. It shows how cash has been generated by or used up in the business. It starts with the profit for the year, as stated by the profit and loss account, and ends with the bank balance shown in the balance sheet.

Well, at least it ought to! I'm afraid that accountants often obscure the message by calling it the source and application of *funds*, not *cash*. They use a different layout from the one I illustrate so you may not recognise my version from the one you will find in most annual accounts.

Professors of accounting theory would say that my *cash* statement oversimplifies the situation for a big company. They are welcome to use statements of source and application of funds which may well be more appropriate for major public companies. For the practical businessman, especially in the smaller one, I contend that they are useless because they not only use incomprehensible jargon but they fail to link the profit to the bank balance clearly.

To see what I mean, I suggest you look at my example on page 85 and compare it with the one in your own accounts. You may find that the statement does not end with the balance in the bank account but with some other total. I find this meaningless. If you do too, try reorganising the figures so that they fit into my layout.

Example of a statement of source and application of cash

Figures in brackets are cash outflows or overdrafts.

Source of Cash		£
Profit for the year before tax		10,000
Add depreciation		5,400
Total from trading		15,400
Sale of fixed assets		—
Loan received		—
Total cash available		15,400

Application of cash

Payments not chargeable against profits

Fixed assets bought (capital expenditure)		(3,000)
Tax paid on profits		(1,800)
Owner's drawings		(6,500)
Net cash left in the business		4,100

Changes in working capital

Current assets:		
Stocks	(Increase) Decrease	(7,250)
Debtors	(Increase) Decrease	(500)
Payments in advance	(Increase) Decrease	(50)
Current liabilities:		
Creditors	Increase (Decrease)	1,700
Advance payments by customers	Increase (Decrease)	—
Cash (used for) or released from working capital		(6,100)
Net increase or (decrease) during year in cash held		(2,000)
Opening cash balance (overdraft)		(16,000)
Closing cash balance (overdraft)		£18,000

You may then find that they make some sense and that they show you clearly what has happened to your money. If you decide you prefer a *cash* statement like mine, I suggest you ask your accountant to produce it. They are your accounts not his, so you are entitled to insist on this.

My example uses the figures for the XYZ shop in Chapters 4 and 5.

Source of cash

We start with the profit for the year before tax from the profit and loss account. We add to it the depreciation for the year. There are two figures for depreciation in the profit and loss account which relate to equipment, fixtures and fittings and to a motor vehicle and the total is £5,400.

The reason that we add depreciation back to the profit, when considering cash flow, is that the figure doesn't represent an actual payment. Money was paid for the assets when they were bought and they are now being written off by depreciation, the latter representing an amount set aside from the profit. If you are unclear about this, see the section on depreciation on page 29.

To the sub-total from trading, we must add cash received which is not reflected in the profit and loss account. Two examples are money in from the sale of fixed assets and from the receipt of a loan.

You may find that your profit and loss account shows either a profit or a loss on the sale of a fixed asset. If it does, you must adjust the profit for the year before tax by deducting the fixed asset profit — or adding back the loss — before entering the figure on the first line. The reason is that a fixed asset profit or loss is the difference between the book value and the money received. It is not the cash itself.

Now we put in the actual money received on the sale of fixed assets line. That figure will not be shown in either the profit and loss account or the balance sheet though you may be able to work it out if the book value of the fixed assets written off is shown, since the cash received must be the book value plus a profit or minus a loss. If not, it will have to come from your detailed records.

In the example, there is no figure to put in because the £200 'sale' is not in fact a sale; it is the value of an item which has been scrapped. Some accountants use the word 'retirements' to mean assets taken out of use which are either scrapped or sold. I regard 'retirements' as more cumbersome and no clearer than 'sale' so I have used the latter in my example.

For loans, you must look at the balance sheet example in the section which follows the one on the profit and loss account. Since the loan has not changed during the year, there has been no cash received and there is nothing to enter.

This means that the total cash available is £15,400.

Application of cash

The lower part of the form then explains how the cash generated by trading was used.

Figures in brackets are minuses
The figures shown in brackets are outflows of cash. Thus fixed assets bought is an actual payment. An increase in stocks represents an outflow because money has had to be paid to finance that increase.

A reduction in debtors represents an inflow and is not in brackets because it means that customers have paid up more promptly so that cash is in the bank instead of being tied up in debtors.

For creditors, the position is the other way round. An increase in creditors means that the latter are lending money on short-term credit to the business. A reduction in creditors means that they have been paid more promptly and there is a corresponding outflow from the bank account.

Payments not chargeable against profits

These figures come from the balance sheet. Your own balance sheet may show the value of the fixed assets bought during the year but, if not, you will find the figure in the attached note on fixed assets. Here it is shown on the face of the balance sheet and the figure is £3,000.

The tax paid on profits is the figure relating to the previous year, not the provision for tax on this year's profits which will not be due until next year. Tax is payable in arrears because it cannot be worked out until the profit is known.

The figure for owner's drawings comes from the balance sheet too. For a limited company, the equivalent is the dividends paid on the share capital and the figure is not shown in the accounts. It has to be worked out from the information they give. During each year, the amount paid is the final dividend for the previous year plus an interim one for the current year — assuming that there is an interim dividend. The final dividend can only be paid after the end of the year because it has first to be approved at the annual general meeting of the company.

Changes in working capital

As explained earlier and in Chapter 11, changes in stocks, debtors, creditors etc either absorb cash or release it. As a business grows, it needs more cash to finance stocks and debtors because higher sales require bigger stocks and larger debtors. Some of the cash is provided by creditors who supply the stocks on credit. Usually, however, the business cannot sell its stocks and collect the money from its customers quickly enough to pay all its creditors on time so it needs extra working capital finance in order to grow.

Alternatively, in a badly managed business, stock and debtors may rise simply because they are not properly controlled.

Here, the figures shown come from the balance sheet and you

can see how I get to them by comparing the 'last year' and 'this year' figures. There is only one detail to note. The increase in creditors includes £200 for future tax payable, the creditor for this having gone up as well as the main creditors total.

As there are no advance payments by customers in this particular balance sheet, there is no entry on that line.

The various minus figures in brackets and the plus figure for finance provided by creditors net to a minus figure in the next line representing cash used for working capital.

Then we compare that minus total with the figure for net cash left in the business on the line higher up and find there is a net decrease in cash held during the year of £2,000. The balance sheet tells us that the starting bank overdraft was £16,000 as shown in the last year column. This enables us to calculate the closing bank overdraft as £18,000. As this agrees with the figure in the balance sheet, the arithmetic is correct.

Thus, the statement of source and application of cash has reconciled the profit from the profit and loss account with the change in the bank balance.

Part 2
How to Use the Figures You Already Have

Chapter 13

How to Get a Grip on Your Cash Position — Now

Is keeping track of your day-to-day cash balance a problem for you? Would you like an immediate feel for the cash position of your business? The cash flow report can give it to you. It's one of the most valuable — perhaps the most important — control documents any business can have.

Do you have answers to these questions at your fingertips?

How much money can you expect to come in over the next month?

How much will you have to pay out?

Where will this leave your bank balance or overdraft?

Will you have enough cash to keep your creditors at bay or will you need to borrow?

What is today's bank balance and is there spare cash at the moment which could go on deposit to earn interest for a week or two?

Will you be able to pay the PAYE/NI contributions and VAT on time?

What are the totals now of your debtors and creditors (accounts receivable and accounts payable)?

If you cannot answer these questions quickly, you do not know enough about your cash flow. You are running the money side of your business blind. This leads to crisis management in which time and energy are wasted in coping with short-term cash problems instead of earning profit.

My cash flow report is the answer. This chapter shows you how to use it to get a grip immediately on the short-term cash situation of any business, whatever its size. I have never seen such a report anywhere else, though I am sure others must had the same idea. It is a simple document which I developed in a situation of dire necessity when, for two and a half years, I ran the finances of a company which was making losses and which was in danger of bankruptcy throughout that period.

The report did not remedy our long-term financial problems but it enabled me to cope with the short-term results of them. It helped me so to manage our meagre resources that we never had a supplier either cut off supplies or refuse us normal trade credit. It showed me how quickly our customers were paying us and I used it also to decide for how much I could authorise my purchase ledger clerk to write cheques to our suppliers each week.

It also showed me what bills were looming up for payment, such as the monthly PAYE/NI contributions and the quarterly VAT. Having the report meant I could not only manage the cash week by week but I could also forecast, one to two months ahead, what our overdraft would be. Not only did we never exceed our limit as a result, in spite of frightful trading difficulties, but I was even able to earn useful interest on short-term deposits for the occasional periods when we had funds in hand, because I knew for how long I could lend the money out.

Two versions of the report are shown: the first is a simplified one suitable for small businesses, especially those which sell services rather than goods. The second is for larger concerns and those which buy goods for resale.

I use the small business version in my consultancy business. It tells me most of the key financial facts of my affairs every Monday morning including my sales, debtors (accounts receivable), expenses and bank balance. It helps me earn extra interest on money, which I put on deposit more quickly because I have the figures at my fingertips each week. It stops me running into an overdraft at the bank unnecessarily by writing cheques for more than the current balance.

It must be the same in your business. If one hasn't got a regular report showing the bank balance, it takes much faffing about to find the paying-in and cheque books and work out a rough one — which tends to be wrong anyway. Somehow, one always needs to know quickly. This report saves me a great deal of time and worry working out whether the money is there when I want to pay a bill. Just how much it had become a part of my way of working and how lost I would be without it I realised recently, when I moved my house and office. With the problems of the move and recruiting a new secretary, my cash flow report slipped for several weeks. I felt financially blind.

The beauty of the report is that it is simple. You'll probably need to adapt my layout to suit your business but, once you've set it up, anyone can extract the figures from your records for you. All they need is common sense, a calculator or, better still, an add/listing machine and access to your sales invoices or sales daybook, if you keep one, your paying-in book and your cheque book. As a bonus, the report will even give you the output figures you need for the dreaded VAT return — so that's part of another problem solved as well!

The main point of the report, however, is to help you manage your money. Whether you need to spin out meagre resources, as I had to in my earlier job, or to earn the maximum interest on spare funds, it will help you too to manage your finances better.

You can produce your first cash flow report today. Once you have got it going, it should not take more than half an hour to do each week, less with practice, especially in a small business. All the figures are available now in your records, however sketchy your accounting system may be, so this powerful tool is yours for the asking.

If you already have a budget for your business, note that the report is not a substitute for an annual cash flow forecast. The latter estimates for a year ahead the cash position month by month on the basis of the budgeted sales and expenses. The cash flow report, on the other hand, works from the actual figures as they happen. Its role is to enable you to control the actual position week by week. The actual totals can then be compared with the budgeted ones so as to enable you to see how close you will be to the latter.

An example of a simple cash flow report

This is the version of the report which I use myself. It is suitable for any service business, ie one which sells time rather than goods, though it may need adapting to suit your precise circumstances. It is intended for those who do not have a full double entry accounting system. If you do, or if you hold stocks of goods for resale, you will probably find the second version on page 100 more suitable but I suggest you skim through this in order to see the general idea.

I round all my figures to the nearest pound except for the VAT. This has to be precise because it is tax due to the government. By including the pence, I can use the weekly totals to give me the quarterly output tax total I need for my VAT return. I do not need pence for the output figure itself — there is no provision for them on the VAT returns. The totals are accurate in spite of not being precise because the rounding tends to cancel out to within a pound or two. Precise figures are an unnecessary nuisance in a report like this because pence take up more space and make it harder to read.

The first line is the value of debtors (accounts receivable) at the beginning of the week. It is the same as the closing debtors from the previous week. If this is the first time you have produced the report, you will have to add up all your outstanding sales invoices to get the total.

A simple cash flow report

	Line	Week 40 £	Week 41 £	Week 42 £	Week 43 £	Cumula-tive position £
Opening debtors	1	8,248	10,756	10,357	8,975	7,967
Invoiced: Consultancy	2	1,464	791	2,990	210	27,855
Seminars	3	118	—	—	—	6,682
Writing	4	1,416	—	—	—	4,469
Subtotal. SR sales	5	2,998	791	2,990	210	39,006
Travel	6	—	50	120	—	2,290
Motor	7	40	—	—	—	420
Telephone	8	25	15	31	8	550
Subtotal; SR outputs	9	3,063	856	3,141	218	42,666
Books ZR	10	105	70	99	105	1,363
Total outputs	11	3,168	926	3,240	323	43,629
VAT	12	459.45	128.40	471.15	32.70	6,340
Total invoiced	13	3,627	1,054	3,711	355	49,969
Less closing debtors	14	10,756	10,357	8,975	7,887	7,887
Money in	15	1,119	1,453	5,093	1,443	50,049
Money out						
Wages/PAYE and NI	16	210			2,337	26,289
Rent	17	54				1,164
Telephone	18					705
Travel	19	95			89	691
Motor	20	79				553
Petty cash	21			79		802
Sundry	22	46			220	1,092
SOs and bank charges	23		2			90
Subtotal; expenses	24	484	2	79	2,646	31,386
Capital expenditure	25		1,500			1,823
Income/corp tax	26				500	500
Drawings	27	20				2,885
VAT paid to C&E	28				1,850	5,218
Deposit account	29				2,000	8,595
Total paid out	30	504	1,502	79	6,996	50,407
Net cash flow	31	615	(49)	5,014	(5,553)	(358)
Opening bank balance	32	665	1,280	1,231	6,245	1,050
Closing bank balance	33	£1,280	£1,231	£6,245	£692	£692

If you have a sales ledger, the total of the account balances is the figure you need. If your ledger is being correctly maintained you will have a sales ledger control account, which will give you the total. In that case I suggest that you check that it agrees with the sum arrived at by listing all the account balances just in case there is an error. It is as well to start with the correct figure.

Next come several lines for the sales invoices issued during the week. I analyse my sales under separate headings for the key parts of my business. Even small businesses can benefit from breaking down their sales into the main categories. Yours might be by department or by location rather than by type of sale. If you have a number of them, it might be better to show the detail on a sub-schedule. I have only a few so I put them all on the main one.

I separate my fee income from expenses recharged to my clients, such as travel, motor and telephone, because these non-profit items otherwise inflate the figures and give a false impression of the real sales. Also I need this analysis for my annual accounts. I like to deduct the recharges from the respective expense headings to show the net cost to me. Doing the analysis this way means more information during the year and less work at the end of it.

The subtotal for standard rated sales, line 5, makes it easy to see my true income total. There's one other income line — for books — which is separate for the reasons explained below.

The subtotal for standard rated outputs, line 9, gives me the figure on which the VAT shown later on line 12 should be 15 per cent — VAT has to be added to expenses recharged as well as to fees. This is a very useful quick check, which proves that both the individual calculations on my invoices and this summary of the figures taken from them are correct. That is valuable because errors in charging VAT can be expensive if the VAT man finds them later when it is too late to collect from the customer. Errors in summarising tax for the return also mean an unexpected bill for extra VAT, if the mistake is against Customs. If it's against you, you have paid too much, which is bad and it might never be found. Often it is possible to protect against errors by laying out one's figures in such a way as to build checks into them and that is what I have done here. It suits my system to check the VAT on the cash flow report but, if you have a separate sales summary, it should be done there.

Books zero rated, line 10, is another income line so, to find my total sales, I must add it to the subtotal for standard rated sales. I cannot avoid that because this line has to be where it is in order to permit the VAT check I have just mentioned.

The total outputs and the VAT lines, numbers 11 and 12, give me figures which I need for my quarterly VAT return. The VAT is a substantial sum and line 12 enables me to keep an eye on the size of the amount I will have to pay. This will be reduced by the input tax I can recover but, in my kind of business, that is fairly small so the output total is a good guide.

The total invoiced, line 13, is the sum of all the invoices I have issued during the week.

When my book-keeper fills in the report, she skips line 14, the closing debtors, for the moment and enters the total of the cash received from debtors during the week on line 15. She then calculates line 14, the debtors outstanding at the end of the week, by deducting line 15 from the total of line 1, starting debtors, and line 13, total invoiced.

The closing debtor figure is an important one in any business — yet many cannot quickly find out how much money they have tied up in it. This report gives me the figure every Monday morning by producing a running total adjusted each week for invoices issued and cash received. There can of course be arithmetical mistakes so we check the total every four or five weeks by adding up all the unpaid invoices themselves. If the total of the unpaid invoices does not agree with the calculated figure we have to look for the error but, with practice, accuracy is not difficult.

If you have a sales ledger, your debtor total each week will come from your sales ledger control account as will the sales invoice and cash received totals. However, like many small businesses, I do not keep a sales ledger. I simply have a file of unpaid invoices, which I have to add up in order to check the calculated total.

If you give cash discounts or issue credit notes to customers, you will need to adjust for these, as shown on the more sophisticated version of the report on page 100.

By comparing the closing debtors with the sales totals including VAT for the previous few weeks, I can keep an eye on how many weeks sales invoices are unpaid and thus how well my credit control system is working. I can also see what cash is likely to come in from my customers in the next week or two since I know the value of the invoices issued a month or so ago.

The next figures in the report are the main expenses which appear in the profit and loss account of my business. Since the number of headings is few, it is easy to show most of them. In a larger business one would lump the smaller ones together, as in the more elaborate example later. The figures come from the cheque book counterfoils or from the cash book, if you keep one.

In my case, 'petty cash', line 21, represents postage and office sundries, the total of which is part of sundry expenses in my accounts. In a larger business it might cover several headings. Which expenses you should show separately depends on which are large enough to matter.

I show standing orders and bank charges at line 23 even though they are small because we do have to remember to pick them up from the bank statement when it comes. Otherwise an error will creep in which will be a nuisance.

The subtotal for expenses at line 24 shows how the total costs are building up. The figures are not the same as the ones which will appear in the profit and loss account because they take no account of opening and closing creditors (accounts payable) or of the adjustments made in the annual accounts for such items as insurance or rates paid in advance. However, these are not very large and, usually being similar to the previous year, they tend to cancel each other out so that the payment totals are a reasonable guide. How true that is for you will depend on how many unpaid bills you usually have.

Next come payments which do not affect the profit and loss account. VAT, capital expenditure and drawings by the owners tend to be large sums relative to the finances of any business. In a limited company, it is important to keep an eye on drawings especially because, if and when the total exceeds any loan account, the cash must be subject to PAYE as salary. One cannot just remove cash when one wants to. It is either a repayment of a loan or it must be taxed. Like most owners of businesses, I pay various private items through my company, often because they are on the same invoice as a business expense. These private amounts are then charged to me as drawings. Showing the figures on line 27 helps me to keep an eye on the total.

In this example, the directors' salaries are included in the wages figure. You might prefer to show them separately from staff pay.

The deposit account, line 30, shows transfers to and from deposit. Thus, in the third week of the example, £2,000 has gone out on deposit. It was transferred in the week after the large influx of cash in order to allow time for the cheques to be cleared. If money is transferred back from the deposit account, it is shown in brackets on line 29.

Line 30 shows the total of all the cheques written each week.

Then we calculate the net cash flow for the week, line 31, by deducting the total paid out, line 30, from the money in, line 15. If the result is a minus, it is in brackets. Brackets show minuses better than red, if you will be photocopying the report. Adjusting the opening cash balance on line 32, which is the same as last week's closing balance, gives me the new bank balance. Overdrafts are also shown in brackets.

Line 32 shows the bank balance as per my books. The bank's records probably show a higher figure on that day due to some cheques not yet having been presented. On the other hand, some of the cheques from customers paid in during the week may not have been collected by the bank so the cleared balance, which is the one on which the bank works when calculating its charges, could be lower. Nevertheless the balance is the same as the one which would appear in a balance sheet drawn up at that date and it is a good working guide.

Two more points: first, the figures build up to totals every four or five weeks, not each calendar month. I do not believe in working in calendar months because of the inconvenience of an end in the middle of the working week. It is much easier in most businesses to run the totals to a weekend. Staff get used to working in accounting weeks more easily and jobs like counting stock or listing unpaid invoices tend to be done more efficiently at the end of a week, especially in a workshop or factory when there is pressure to get the work out. I therefore recommend that you divide the year into four 13-week quarters each of which subdivides into two four- and one five-week periods.

The cumulative totals give me an indication of my profit for the year to date. Whether it will do so in your business depends on how many other complications you have. The report is a better guide to profit in a service business than in one which has money tied up in stocks of goods for sale or work in progress. If you are not sure why changes in stock levels do not affect cash in the same way as profit, see Chapter 11.

Depreciation and bad debts are not shown so one has to allow for these when using the report as a guide to profit.

The second point is that the figures reveal patterns after one or two periods. For instance, salaries and PAYE/NI payments appear regularly at intervals. It could be important to show the total paid out to employees separately from the PAYE/NI. I do not bother but, for many businesses the monthly PAYE/NI cheque is significant. A separate line highlights whether or not it has been sent.

Other bills like VAT, electricity and telephone appear quarterly. This helps one to assess the position at a glance not only as of today but over the next month or two. The pattern of payments shows what major bills, such as VAT, are due shortly.

The report thus helps to avoid those unpleasant surprises which result if you overlook such a payment when relying on your bank statement. Not only does the report help one to control the cash properly, it saves much waste of time in checking up on whether key bills have been paid.

A cash flow report suitable for those who sell goods

The cash flow report I use in my business will suit many other small ones, though it omits certain information which may be important to you and it includes some detail which you may not need. The next example is more appropriate for a business which sells goods. It may suit you better or you could use part of both reports adapted to suit your needs.

This version is intended to be completed weekly, like the one already discussed. However, only the period totals are shown in the example, in order to fit the year to date figures for actual and budget on the page of this book. This shows how the report can be compared with your budget, if you have one. Incidentally, I see no point in comparing the period totals with the budget for that period. Differences in the timing of payments are inevitable. It is the totals for the year to date which matter.

The report begins as before with opening debtors and invoices issued. At line 4, it shows the deductions from sales needed if you allow cash discounts to customers. You might also want a line for credit notes issued to customers if you take goods back or if you have to adjust your customer's accounts for short deliveries, breakages etc.

There is a separate line, number 6, for cash sales because some businesses have a retail counter or sell for spot cash to some customers or to staff, as well as making sales on credit.

The lines 8 and 9 for other receipts can be important when assets are regularly sold off, loans are received, or there are other exceptional receipts, which must not be confused with ordinary income. For instance, you would use the 'other' line, number 9, for money which you put into the business yourself.

Now we come to a new part of the report, at line 11, which is not in the more simple version. In many businesses, the total owed to creditors is an important figure. If you buy goods for resale, you are sure to need the information provided by this part of the report.

You get the figures in much the same way as those for debtors and sales. The opening creditors total is the closing one from last week or, when starting to use the form, the total of the balances on your purchase ledger, if you have one, or of your unpaid invoices

THE ZYX CO
Monthly cash flow report

4 weeks ended 30 September

Figures in brackets are minuses or overdrafts

	Line	Period actual £	Year to date Actual £	Year to date Budget £
Opening debtors	1	1,800	1,000	1,000
Add: Sales on credit inc VAT	2	1,600	4,700	3,600
Less: Closing debtors	3	(1,900)	(1,900)	(1,000)
Discounts allowed	4	(—)	(—)	(—)
Cash received from debtors	5	1,500	3,800	3,600
Cash sales inc VAT	6	3,600	11,500	11,000
Total cash from sales	7	5,100	15,300	14,600
Other receipts: Assets sold	8	—	200	200
Other	9	—	1,000	1,000
Total cash in	10	5,100	16,500	15,800
Opening creditors	11	2,050	1,300	1,300
Add: Bought ledger invoices inc VAT	12	3,500	12,250	10,600
Less: Closing creditors	13	(1,150)	(1,150)	(1,300)
Payments made — Bought ledger	14	4,400	12,400	10,600
— Cash items	15	1,380	3,560	4,200
Total cash out	16	5,780	15,960	14,800
Net cash flow	17	(680)	540	,1000
Opening bank balance	18	(1,780)	(3,000)	(3,000)
Closing bank balance	19	(2,460)	(2,460)	(2,000)

Analysis of total cash out				
Net wages		90	280	420
NI and PAYE		—	—	
Rent		—	260	260
Electricity		60	60	60
Telephone		—	20	20
Loan interest		—	50	50
VAT		270	270	270
Rates		—	290	29C
Bank charges and interest		—	—	—
Insurance		—	100	100
Capital expenditure		—	500	1,000
Drawings		250	800	800
Income/Corporation tax		600	600	600
Petty cash		30	150	—
All other (inc goods and expenses)		4,480	12,580	10,930
Total cash out		5,780	15,960	14,800

from suppliers if you do not.

The invoices total comes from the purchase ledger control account or the purchase invoice day book if you have such records. If you do not, you will need to add up all the purchase invoices you received on credit during the week. Ignore for now any invoices which you paid immediately (see line 15) — just list those for goods or services which you bought on credit.

Then you jump to line 14, just as you did in dealing with debtors and sales above. You enter the total of the cheques written in the week to pay invoices received on credit. Then you calculate the closing creditors the same way as you did the closing debtors.

Most businesses pay a few bills immediately on receipt and these are not therefore entered in the purchase ledger. Line 15 is for the total of these cheques.

If you do not have a purchases ledger, you might find it easier not to have to separate the 'immediate' payments from those for purchases on credit. You can avoid having to do so by including *all* invoices received in the figure on line 12. Line 15 is then unnecessary, all payments being shown on line 14.

The same remarks concerning accuracy apply as for the closing debtors figure in my comments on the simpler version of the report. It does not matter if there are minor errors or omissions. The key point is to have before one every Monday morning the approximate totals of what one owes and is owed.

The *pattern* of purchase invoice totals can be especially useful if the business has a heavy programme of either capital investment or seasonal stock building. However carefully one tries to estimate the timing, a cash flow forecast made a year ahead can only be a guess. The cash flow report shows how the invoices are actually coming in, thus providing accurate information a month or so before the cash to pay them has to be found.

The remaining lines for net cash flow and the bank balance are completed in the same way as for the simpler version.

This version of the report omits the detail of the payments, which is shown on the simpler one. The reason is that to analyse the payments on the same sheet of paper would crowd the layout and make it more difficult to read.

I believe it is preferable to show the totals as per the example and to have a second sheet giving the payments in whatever detail is appropriate to your business. You do not need to show all the expense headings. I suggest you show the significant sums which are either easy to pick out, like the weekly or monthly salaries cheque, or are irregular, like capital expenditure, or are paid at intervals, like insurance. A suggested payments analysis is on page 100.

You may wish to adapt these examples anyway to produce your own version of the report to suit your circumstances. For instance you, might want to show output and input VAT separately from sales and purchase invoices on the second example to see how the net balance is building up.

Any business can have a weekly cash flow report. The figures needed are readily available whatever the state of your records. The effort required to produce it is minimal, yet it imposes a useful discipline in ensuring that key figures are added up each week. The report offers the following valuable information about the business:

- ☐ Your sales to date.
- ☐ How much your customers owe you — assuming you sell on credit.
- ☐ How much you owe your suppliers — if significant enough to be included in the report.
- ☐ How much cash you are likely to receive from customers and/or will have to pay out to suppliers over the next month — from the pattern of sales and purchase invoice totals.
- ☐ The totals of your costs paid out to date — which in many businesses will be a fair indication of how they are building up.
- ☐ If you do not hold significant stocks or work in progress, the report will often be a reasonable guide to your profit to date — before depreciation on fixed assets or bad debts, of course.
- ☐ Your bank balance — after taking into account all cheques written and all money banked up to date.

Action to be taken

This chapter has shown two versions of the cash flow report, one of the most valuable business tools in managing a business. Whether your business is simple or complicated, one of the examples can be adapted to suit it. However chaotic your records, all the information you need is available for a minimum of effort. In my business, all my staff have to do is to add up the figures on the sales invoices for the week's sales and to note the money in from the paying-in book and the payments from the cheque book counter-foils. The rest is a few minutes' arithmetic. What could be simpler?

So, no questions on this chapter — action! How about getting out your records now and drawing up your own report? Once you've got the routine going, someone can do the figures for you each

Monday morning. The improved knowledge of your finances and the peace of mind which comes from having things under control will repay a hundredfold the effort to get it going. I know. I'm a qualified accountant; yet I muddled along without the report for ages before I made myself do it. Now I wouldn't be without it.

Chapter 14

How to Get Your Customers to Pay up More Quickly

Why it matters

If you sell on credit, there's always too much money tied up in debtors (accounts receivable). The tank chart in Chapter 11 showed you how cash is absorbed this way. To defeat the tendency for debtors to use too much of your money will require your best efforts and most earnest attention. It will be worth it because, together with stocks of goods, this aspect of your business will soak up cash quicker than any other if you let it. Many others do let it. Letting customers borrow too much money by not enforcing payment on time is expensive and often restricts a business's ability to invest in its future.

For example, suppose your sales including value added tax for the last three months were as follows:

	£
Jan	30,000
Feb	40,000
March	30,000
	£100,000

Your invoices are due for payment 30 days after their date of issue so, theoretically, only the March ones should be unpaid on 1 April, value £30,000.

Suppose your customers in reality take on average two and a half months' credit; the figure will in fact be £85,000, ie March plus February plus half the January invoices. So your customers have £55,000 more of your money than they should.

Worse still, if your sales are standard-rated at 15 per cent, and your VAT quarter ends on 31 March, a month later on 30 April, you will have to pay the government the VAT on the March and half the February sales which you will still not have collected. Since the figures include VAT, that means a further drain of 3/23 × £70,000 = £9,130.

A good credit control system has a vital part to play in ensuring that the money comes in when it should because, if you do not ask for your money on time and you do not make a fuss if you do not get it, customers will get the message that you do not mind.

Bad credit control costs a bomb!

1. You pay interest on a higher overdraft or fail to earn it on deposit.
2. Chase-up letters cost money plus time of staff who could be better employed on more productive tasks.
3. Your bad debts are higher because they do not get spotted early. Not only do some become bad merely because you are last rather than first to be paid, but you probably go on supplying long after a good system would have warned you to stop throwing good money after bad.
4. Money in debtors, which ought to be in the bank, cannot be used to develop the business.

Let's have the right information
First, work out what the value of your debtors ought to be, using the sales figures for the last few months, not the annual average. Seasonal variations often make averages meaningless.

Add VAT, if applicable, to the sales figures since it is included in the sums owed to you.

Adjust also for credit balances on your sales ledger — amounts owed by you to customers rather than owed by them to you. Often the balances are artificial, being the result of accounting errors or special situations, and the total may be large enough to distort the statistics. Show the gross sums owed to you and any credit balances owed by you as separate totals. The true position will probably be shown by using the gross total for your statistics, not the net one.

If there are any large customers who pay on special terms, whether very quickly or more slowly than the rest, it may be necessary to eliminate both sales to them and the amounts outstanding from them from the totals of sales and debtors in order to see the true picture for the majority to whom your normal terms apply. Export customers are often an example of those to whom special extended credit terms apply, if only because of the delays in collecting money in foreign currencies around the world.

Having found out the true position as to how many days' sales are outstanding you can then measure the difference on what it ought to be and can assess how serious the problem is and therefore how much attention it merits.

In any case, you will not remedy a bad situation overnight. If your customers are used to taking two and a half months' credit, they will have to be retrained. This can be done by adopting a firm policy properly enforced but it will take time to cajole, persuade or threaten them into paying on time. How long will depend upon your industry and your relationships generally with your customers but, inevitably, they won't like being asked to stop keeping your money longer than they should and some may take umbrage.

However, the risk of offending customers by requiring prompt payment is a short-term one. Once they know your policy and that you mean to enforce it, customers are usually willing to pay more or less on time. Generally speaking, not much worthwhile business is obtained by allowing long credit. The bad payers tend not to be worth having as customers.

The need for a policy on credit terms

Getting your debtors to pay up on time demands careful attention to detail. Have a policy on credit. Set time limits and make sure your customers and your staff understand them. Show the terms on price-lists, invoices and statements, and write welcoming letters to new customers quoting them.

Good credit control is largely a matter of habit on the part of both your customers and your staff. If your customers know that you expect them to pay promptly they are much more likely to do so than if you often let matters drag on. This is especially true in organisations big enough to employ clerks to process invoices. These staff soon get to know who presses them for payment and who does not and they tend to set their priorities accordingly. Well, you would too in their place! Don't be intimidated by large organisations, however. Their different departments usually do not talk to each other much. One can often make personal contact with the accounts staff who can ensure payment of invoices without in any way affecting the relationship with the buyer.

Are your credit terms clear?

Wording such as 'Net monthly' or 'Payment is due on the 21st of the month following' is vague and an invitation to your customers to interpret it in their favour. Be precise, with wording like 'Payment should be received by us within 30 days of the date of this invoice' or 'Payment of all invoices should be received by us not later than the 21st of the month following that in which they are dated'. Perhaps you can shorten the above while remaining specific but there is too much money at stake for brevity to be the main consideration.

Print the terms clearly on your invoices and statements, on your acknowledgements of orders too if you have them, so that they cannot be missed. Do not hide them apologetically in a corner as if they do not really matter!

Credit limits

If you sell regularly to the same people, set limits for credit to individual customers and see that your sales records show when a limit is being exceeded. This is especially important for new customers but it can also be a useful protection against something suddenly going wrong with a long-established one who pays regularly. If you use a computer, it may be able to calculate automatically a limit based upon average orders for each account for the last six months, say. A balance exceeding the limit then triggers a signal prompting a check on the circumstances.

Control in the order office

Put your policy in writing to the staff in the order office who must prevent goods going out to overdue accounts. Organise a system for producing up-to-date details of those who are over their credit limits or who are on the 'stop' list for non-payment, *and enforce it*! Do not go on handing out goods or services to customers whose silence already indicates that they may not be going to pay.

In every industry there is a hard core of undesirable customers who run up bills with any supplier who allows them to do so. Then, when the supplier finally stops deliveries, they move on to some other source of easy credit. Once gone, they never come back.

By being tough, you minimise such losses and you may even retain some of this floating business.

Opening new accounts

The sales staff must understand the credit terms, upon what basis they can open new credit accounts, and whose authority is required.

The moment a new customer asks for credit is the time when he can be asked for references etc. The minimum information which should be asked for is as follows:

Is he a sole trader, partnership or limited company?
Who are the owners/partners/directors?
How long in business?
Full address and telephone number.
If a new business, what is previous career of the principals?
What is the nature of the business?
If a limited company, is a guarantee of the directors available?
Or up-to-date accounts?
If a new business, how is it being financed?
What trade references are available?
What credit limit is needed to cover the expected business?

Vary this list of questions to suit your trade. It may seem formidable but in practice potential customers often appreciate the efficiency of the supplier who does take the trouble to check them out. It is particularly important to know the background of a limited company. These tend to have a spurious credibility because of the 'limited'. In practice, since the liability to creditors is indeed limited, doing business with them is often riskier than with a sole trader or a partnership.

Trade references can be valuable, particularly if they are from people in the same business as yourself. Do not be afraid to approach a competitor for an 'off the record' chat about a potential new customer. Often there is cooperation on credit because everyone has the same problem.

Beware of references given by the prospective customer. Many bad payers keep a few accounts up to date especially for use as references.

There are various trade protection societies and credit reference organisations who will supply information about customers, such as credit ratings, latest accounts filed if a limited company and so on. Try Yellow Pages or your Chamber of Commerce for local addresses. The London based national organisations advertise in such media as the *Financial Times*.

The Registrar of Companies, Companies House, Crown Way, Maindy, Cardiff CF4 3UZ; telephone 0222 388588, will supply a copy of the latest filed accounts of a company. At the time of writing, the fee is £3 per enquiry.

Get your bills out quickly

Get your invoices out as soon as possible after you have delivered the goods or done the work. It looks efficient and customers like confirmation of the price. Moreover until he has your invoice, the customer cannot approve it and put it into his payment system.

Can you make it easy for him to pay by including a payment slip, possibly a Giro one? Ask your bank for details of the Giro system.

Then get the statement out promptly and follow up as soon as the credit period is exceeded. Keep following up! Monthly intervals are much too long. My father used to say, 'Send them a postcard daily!' He exaggerated, but not by that much. Debtors soon notice at what intervals you chase them. Depending on your credit terms, a monthly statement should be followed by a polite overdue reminder a few days or at most two weeks later. Subsequent letters should be at weekly or fortnightly intervals — not three, four or more weeks later. The psychological effect of rapid follow-up is to convince the debtor that you really mean business, that you care about getting your money.

On the other hand, slow follow-up creates the opposite impression: that you do not mind that much, that it does not matter.

A debtor's willingness to pay is at its maximum in the initial credit period. It then declines rapidly as the bill becomes more and more overdue. Before long the debtor begins to feel he or she does not really owe the money and to resent attempts to collect it. This is psychological. I expect you've been a debtor in that situation. I have. So ask for your money promptly and keep on asking. Asking first often means being paid first.

All this, of course, requires an efficient accounting system capable of producing the necessary figures and details on time so that you can ask for your money.

How we do it in my business

An efficient system is not necessarily an elaborate one. In my business, we do not have a sales ledger with account cards for each customer. A ledger is really only needed if you have a lot of transactions with each customer, possibly involving credit notes for returns etc. Then the detail becomes hard to follow unless the transactions are all grouped together in a ledger account.

I simply have my secretary type three copies of each invoice. The customer gets the top copy; the second goes in numerical order on to the sales invoice file; the third goes on to the unpaid invoices file. When the invoice is paid, we write the date the cheque is received on the third copy which is then transferred to a paid invoices file. To see which invoices are outstanding, I therefore have to look through one file only, the oldest invoices being at the back.

We follow up first with a 'Have you forgotten?' sticker on a photocopy of the invoice 30 days after its date. Two weeks after this gentle reminder we send a brief letter signed by my book-keeper or my secretary, which they sign; it gives them a little status and encourages them to operate the system. Chasing up is not delayed if I am away.

If after another two weeks, ie two months after the date of the invoice, it is still unpaid, we start getting upset. My staff telephone rather than write. So far I have not been involved, which means that I can now intervene if necessary either by telephone or in writing with a plaintive, 'My staff tell me my bill is unpaid. Is there a problem?'

Chasing the bad payers

If this all fails to get results, I do not mess about. I either put the matter into the hands of a collection agency or, if the debtor is a limited company, I threaten to apply to the court to have it wound up using wording similar to the following:

> We write in respect of the outstanding amount of £XX for (state nature of goods or services you supplied) pursuant to our invoice dated . . .. Despite repeated requests for payment including a letter on . . . and a telephone call on . . ., you have neglected to pay the amount due.
>
> Accordingly we give you notice that if the amount of £XX is not paid to us within three weeks from receipt by you of this letter we are to commence proceedings to wind up the Company on the basis of Section 223 of the Companies Act, 1948.
>
> Yours faithfully

If that does not produce a response, the threat can only be carried out once various formalities have been complied with and there are costs involved in doing so. You cannot use s. 223 for a debt under £200 and it may not be suitable for use in a dispute in which your customer denies he owes you money, so you should take legal advice if you think you may have to take the required action. However, the threat itself is often enough to obtain payment or to extract the facts when a customer has been stalling because he is in financial difficulties.

This is not a text book on credit control and the law so, for information on how to sue your debtors in the courts, go to your lawyer, a specialist book or one of the debt collection agencies.

Everyone has some slow payers. I maintain that the longer they are left, the slower they will pay, if they pay at all. So I repeat, asking first often means being paid first: pressing for payment quicker than other suppliers will at least prevent you throwing good money after bad and it may mean that you are the one who gets paid. Discover the bad news as soon as you can. You may even be able to help your customer by making a sensible arrangement under which he pays off the debt while you continue to supply against cash on delivery.

Train your staff

Credit control is often a junior function with low grade staff. Train them. Do not let sales and marketing dominate with all attention on getting and filling orders and none on obtaining payment. Your staff need to know you care about credit control before you can expect them to operate a tight system. Yet once they are properly trained and motivated, they can do most of the work for you.

If your clerks are to chase customers for payment without giving offence, they must be taught how. Good liaison with other departments is essential so they know if there are any reasons for delayed payment such as disputed or incomplete deliveries, quality problems etc. A pleasant telephone manner and an ability to write good letters are important. The way your people ask for payment can improve or undermine your image, just as much as the salesman who visits.

In particular, complaints which your follow-up system unearths should be documented and dealt with efficiently. Do you have an analysis of complaints on which to base effective query control and remedial action? Are your people trained to press for the balance of the money not in question, leaving just the disputed amount unpaid?

Cash discounts

Giving cash discounts is a poor substitute for good credit control.

The true cost of a discount of 2½ per cent for payment at 30 days is the price reduction related to the number of days by which payment is received earlier. So, if customers would normally pay at 65 days on average, the calculation is:

$$\frac{2.5}{97.5} \times \frac{365}{35} = 26.7\%$$

This is an expensive way to obtain prompt payment. And do your customers really take 65 days? Suppose it is 45 days on average and you allow three days of grace for the discount, you only get your money 12 days earlier. Then the real cost of the discount is:

$$\frac{2.6}{97.5} \times \frac{365}{12} = 78\%$$

Similar calculations apply to 3.75 per cent at 7 days for which, usually, the true period in practice is 10 days. If your customers would pay net on average at 45 days anyway, your interest cost is:

$$\frac{3.75}{96.25} \times \frac{365}{35} = 40.6\%$$

Many companies have found that an efficient invoicing, credit control and cash collection system can reduce debtors and cut credit periods without any need to offer cash discounts. If you offer them, ask yourself whether you have to for some reason or whether you could cut them out. That you may have always offered a discount and that most others in your trade do so are not sound reasons for continuing the practice, given the high cost.

Interest on overdue accounts

To threaten to charge interest on an overdue account is not usually a very effective means of obtaining prompt payment in practice. The rate charged must of course be very high or customers may simply use you as a lender!

If your claim for interest is to be enforceable in law, the terms must be clearly notified to your customer in advance. This means, at the very least, showing them on your order acceptance stationery or in correspondence regarding the order as well as on invoices and statements.

Dealing with major companies

Do not hesitate to apply your normal procedures simply because the customer is a household name. Remember Rolls-Royce went down! It may not be appropriate to ask for trade references or annual accounts but you should certainly find out who will be responsible for approving your bill and where the purchase ledger is located. Make contact with the customer's chief accountant or whoever is in charge of payment accounts and politely make the point about your terms of business at the start.

Some major companies take extra credit from small companies as a matter of policy. Check with other small traders in your area on their experience. Submit your bills promptly — a big organisation genuinely needs more time to approve and process them for payment — and as soon as delays occur, make a fuss.

Major orders can bankrupt you

A prospective customer, a big company perhaps a household name, enquires for a substantial quantity of goods. The potential business is tremendous — perhaps a quarter or more of your existing turnover — but of course they do have their own specifications which you must meet.

You are excited. You 'leap about', invest time in technical development and produce some samples. The reaction of the customer is enthusiastic. You investigate the production problems, spend hours with the customer's technical staff, more time, and probably money in perfecting the technical process.

It looks great. The order is practically in the bag. It just has to go up to the Buying Committee at the customer's headquarters, but his technical staff and his buyer assure you that there will be no problem. Meanwhile, how soon can you start production?

You now really get going. You order in materials, take your staff off other tasks to plan the operation. You buy new equipment and mention a fur coat to the wife. Everything's running smoothly — your organisation has turned itself upside down to meet the challenge but you're ready to start next month — as soon as you get the order.

You never do get the order. At the customer's HQ the proposals are turned down — a change of policy, new buyer, technical problems — the reasons hardly matter, you're not going to get the order.

And you've spent money on research and development, materials in quantities you cannot use, equipment now not needed — without any commitment by the customer! Tough!

It happens to others regularly; do not get caught by this kind of 'bad debt'. As soon as material sums of money and/or time are involved, ask for money. It might be a contribution to costs or a commitment to pay them or a firm order. What matters is a legal obligation at least to see you do not lose money. Get it in writing — the executive you are dealing with may not have authority to place orders and asking for a written commitment will force any problem into the open. Don't place firm orders for materials or equipment until you have one yourself.

One businessman I know takes his accountant along once negotiations start on the financial aspects of a deal. The accountant looks severe and says 'no' at critical moments. Not a bad discipline as well as a good negotiating ploy!

Tell the salesman what's happening

The salesman's function is to sell but he should do so intelligently. Make sure that he understands the reasons for having credit terms and that he is able to justify them to customers. It is better to avoid using him to collect money unless this is normal trade practice, because it may be more difficult for him to get appointments if the customer knows that a cheque will be asked for. Moreover, if the system depends upon your salesman calling, any delay or missed dates due to sickness, holidays etc slows up the money coming in. If the salesman only calls, say, every six weeks that is serious because his failure to do so provides the perfect excuse for your customer not to write that cheque.

Do see, however, that your salesmen are aware of your slow payers. It is hard for them if they call unawares on an account just after the customer has had a confrontation with your accounts staff.

The salesman's authority to vary credit terms must be clear

It is up to you to decide, in the circumstances of your business, whether to let your salesman allow extra credit. In most businesses, it is better not to because of the clash of priorities this creates. The natural tendency of all salesmen is to sell however they can and to permit them to give extended credit is likely to be a very expensive way of getting orders.

However, it can pay off to make exceptions for customers starting up or short of cash for some special reason. Here creative credit control can sometimes build a customer into a larger account with a long-term loyalty to you because of the way you helped him in the early days.

If salesmen are authorised to propose longer credit in such special cases, the deal should be subject to approval by the office. Put it in writing and explain that it is a temporary concession, state the payment dates agreed and limit the period and/or value involved.

Do your salesmen update your account details?

How many of *your* suppliers irritate *you* by invoicing you with the name of your business incomplete or wrong, with silly errors in the address or even in the name of the previous owner or occupier of the premises? Often the problem starts because sales staff do not inform the office when a business changes hands or because orders are carelessly made out.

If your own invoices contain such errors, this is bound to aggravate your credit control problems, if not actually to cause bad debts. How can you sue a business if you do not have the correct name?

Can your order forms or other sales stationery include a box for confirming or correcting the invoicing details?

Bad debts are no good to anyone

Remember that a sale on credit is not complete until you are paid. Bad debts not only lose you the value of goods supplied plus the VAT charged but also cost money to administer. A sale which is not paid for is better not made.

Suppose that you work on a gross profit margin of 20 per cent. A bad debt of £115 will therefore have cost you £80-worth of goods plus VAT of £15 on the value of the sale. To recover that £95 you will have to make further sales of £475 or *five times the loss*.

Credit insurance

You can insure against bad debts. Trade Indemnity Ltd, 34 Great Eastern St., London EC2A 3AX; tel. 01-739 4311, charges 20p to 50p per £100 or 80 per cent of the risk. The fees are variable according to amounts and periods of credit to your major customers.

The Export Credits Guarantee Department, Aldermanbury House, Aldermanbury Square, London EC2P 2EL; tel 01-382 7000, provides cover for overseas. Apart from protecting you against up to 95 per cent of your loss, ECGD can help with advice on the creditworthiness of foreign countries and customers.

Do you export?

Apart from the services of ECGD mentioned above, there are

various aspects of financing foreign credit to be considered.

You will need to learn about letters of credit and bills of exchange, for instance. Ask your bank for advice. Ask them also about the various ways in which payment can be collected from overseas.

For instance, in whose currency will the letter of credit or bill be stated? In which country will it be payable and at what bank?

Some banks are much better at collecting money from overseas than others. The American banks have sometimes been the best. The English clearing banks have often been appallingly slow. The position varies according to the country involved and it is changing as a result of increased competition so it may pay to ask round. Do not necessarily rely on your domestic bank.

These may seem minor technical points but they can have a considerable effect on how much cash is tied up in export deals and for how long.

Summary

Good credit control is good business management and your customers will appreciate it as much as you do. The best of them prefer to deal with efficient suppliers and do not resent being held to terms of business providing that those terms are fair, in accordance with normal trade practice, and are clearly understood by them. This applies to discounts or to any other aspect of credit.

Sometimes it is indeed possible to retain a customer and help him to build his business by refusing him credit. This may prevent him from overtrading and may make him run his affairs that much more efficiently so that he stays in business and remains your customer.

There is no quicker way of losing customers than to allow them to take extended credit and then have to chase them for it, whereupon they go to other suppliers. In the long run little worthwhile business is obtained by being too easy on credit.

Success in minimising the cash tied up in debtors demands a good system, carefully thought out and systematically applied.

Chapter 15

How to Control Your Money Tied up in Stocks

In many businesses stocks of goods for resale or of materials for use in the business are one of the biggest figures in the balance sheet. If this is so in your business, failure to control the amount of money tied up in your stocks could sink you.

Stock control is a big subject. Many businesses have elaborate systems based upon sophisticated techniques. Computers and other electronic equipment are making possible far more detailed control even for small companies. This is not a dissertation on these systems — just a collection of common-sense points and hints for the practical manager on what causes excess stock and how to avoid it, especially in the smaller business.

Clever systems are a great help in controlling stock but common sense and simple good management will always be more important. All the systems can do is provide information about the results of the way you manage your stock. They may help you take decisions but they cannot make them for you.

Why stock control matters

Stock eats up cash faster than any other aspect of a business. The tank chart on page 77 shows you how this happens. It is easier to buy goods than to sell them (except for antiques) so there are always some items which sell slowly, if at all. Since the mistakes remain and the successes have to be replaced with more of the same, one's stock tends to get bigger and bigger. If uncontrolled this results in more and more money being tied up in lines which you cannot sell until, one day, you run out of money to restock with the ones you can.

As a general proposition, holding stock is bad news

People sometimes kid themselves that holding stock is a worthwhile 'investment'. Normally that cannot be true. It may be when inflation is in double figures or when there are shortages of goods or materials, but only for *some* items. Extra purchases of these may pay off either because of the extra profit from inflated selling prices, or increased business resulting from being able to hold prices while stocks last, or because the goods may be unobtainable later.

The problem is to know *which* items will pay off. However severe inflation is, there are always some goods which do not sell even if the original price is maintained. As for supposed shortages, buying ahead of your needs is speculating. If you want to gamble on commodity prices, fine, but do not kid yourself that it is a normal business operation.

The one exception to the general rule of buying only for your immediate needs is when your business relies on a key component which you expect to be in short supply and which is produced by only a few sources. Microchips are a possible example, for a manufacturer who uses them in his products.

Of course you must have adequate stocks to supply your customers. The problem is how to minimise the cost of doing this, given that the money tied up not only earns no interest but tends to lose value.

There are too many causes of stock wastage for stockholding to be other than an expensive exercise in most cases.

How stock loses its value

The expense of holding stock has been estimated at 25 per cent of its cost each year, allowing for interest on the money tied up and wastage. Some causes of wastage are:

☐ *Damage* in handling — especially in stockrooms which are over-crowded.

☐ *Deterioration* during long storage — dusty packaging can make an item unsaleable for instance.

☐ *Evaporation* and other natural reductions in quantity or quality.

☐ *Obsolescence.* You no longer make the product of which it was part, your supplier has updated the product or there is a new product which does the same job better. Computer games are an example of rapid obsolescence as more elaborate ones are invented and the computers themselves are altered.

☐ *Changes in fashion.* Women's clothes are only one example. Fads come and go for things such as home snooker tables and skateboards: and who remembers the hula hoop?

☐ *Over-buying.* You buy too many because you overestimate sales, cout your stock wrongly, overlook a parcel of stock or duplicate an order. As a result stock is held past its 'sell by' date or the season ends.

☐ *Pilferage.* Customers, staff and delivery drivers will all take your goods without paying if you put temptation their way by not having good controls. Obviously the more stock you have, the easier it is for some to get 'lost' without it being noticed.

The problem of pilferage

Pilferage takes many forms from outright theft, such as shoplifting, to minor misuse by employees such as writing private letters on company stationery or using equipment, vehicles etc, for private purposes. Often staff regard such use as a perk of the job and it may be tolerated or even accepted as such by the employer.

The problem starts with you, the boss. If you do not show you care, you cannot expect employees to mind, even if they are honest decent people.

Showing you care means devoting time to sensible controls both physical and on paper. Valuable stocks should be locked away and access restricted, all goods being booked out.

In a tobacconist's shop, for instance, the owner cannot record sales off the shelves but he can note the number of packs of 200 cigarettes taken from the stockroom to the shelves. Similarly a publican can record the issue of bottles of spirits to his bars.

Such records make it much harder for complete packs or whole bottles to disappear. In many businesses similar records can do much to reduce the risk of theft if only because they demonstrate that the management cares. The problem, of course, is to draw the line between paperwork which is worth doing and that which simply creates work. Part of the answer lies in concentrating upon the more valuable and more attractive items. By establishing some checks on your goods you can do much to reduce temptation and keep people honest. If on the other hand, you presume upon their honesty, you will have trouble sooner or later.

Watch those delivery men

Those who deliver goods to you must be controlled just as carefully as your customers or your staff. Never allow them to off-load goods direct into your stockroom. Ideally you should have a separate reception area so that there is no possibility of incoming goods being mixed up with stocks or with despatches to customers. Goods arriving should either be checked at once or should be signed for as 'unexamined'.

119

Here are some of the ways in which many delivery drivers regularly fiddle other people. Do not let them do it to you!

- ☐ If the quantity off-loaded is not checked, driver retains a parcel on the vehicle or, in the case of, say petrol or oil, the tank on the vehicle is either not emptied or is not full in the first place. If the quantity is checked, the driver off-loads the correct amount but picks up a parcel and puts it back on the vehicle when the checker's back is turned.
- ☐ If access to the parcels is possible, driver extracts part of contents prior to delivery.
- ☐ If goods come in different qualities, driver delivers lower grade than ordered, then sells better grade elsewhere, possibly splitting the difference with another customer who ordered the lower grade.
- ☐ If driver collects empty containers for credit, a smaller quantity is recorded than is uplifted. Or a crate of full ones is removed instead of empties.

Stock inefficiency

Too much stock takes up valuable space, makes it difficult to bring in new lines, change policies to meet new conditions etc. It may even clutter your premises so much that you cannot find items when they are wanted.

Hidden costs of stockholding

Thus excess stock can generate many hidden costs, lose you opportunities due to shortage of space or cash, and generally reduce the efficiency of your business. It simply does not pay to tie up more money in stock than you have to.

Basic rules of stockholding

1. Keep a tidy, well ordered stockroom laid out to a system. Allocate space according to gross *profit* generated (*not* gross sales *value*).
2. Keep records of stock and orders placed so that you have facts upon which to base each order.
3. Do not leave the ordering of fresh supplies to junior staff. Orders prepared by them on the basis of past sales should be scrutinised by someone who can assess future demand and

is aware of plans for new products etc which may affect the need to reorder. A routine order for materials involves spending a substantial sum. Yet in many businesses, a clerk can place such an order whereas a new desk costing a fraction of its value requires the authorisation of the boss.

Since surplus materials may be difficult to sell or even valueless to anyone else whereas the desk can always be sold off quickly, the priorities are all wrong.

Why surplus stock gets bought in the first place

Some of the causes are:

☐ Failure to match purchasing and/or production to sales, ie continuing to buy in normal quantities when demand has started to drop or when a product is to be discontinued or suspended.

☐ The 'just in case' syndrome. 'We had better have a few just in case someone wants one.' This attitude is typical of factory staff or shop managers if they get criticised for failure to meet demand but receive no praise for keeping stocks low.

☐ If the factory needs long production runs in order to be efficient, a standard run may take far too long if the line is slow selling.

☐ Buying in quantity to obtain cheaper prices. This is rarely worth while and can amount to commodity speculation, as already mentioned. See the story about table lighters below.

Do you make sure suppliers deliver when scheduled, not before?

Suppose you order 10,000 units of a container for your product to be delivered over the next five months at 2,000 per month. So as to minimise his production cost, your supplier will probably produce all 10,000 in a single run. You do not want them all now partly because you do not have enough space for them and partly because you have agreed to pay on delivery.

At your supplier's factory however, they too are short of space. Maybe their foreman decides to put 5,000 on a lorry for delivery to you, not 2,000. If your goods reception system is not adequate to identify the over-delivery of 3,000 and your staff do not realise what is happening, they will probably allow the driver to off-load the surplus. The result is not only an overcrowded stockroom but also an invoice for 5,000 units due now, not 2,000. Even if you spot the try-on at this stage, you are in a weak position, having taken delivery.

How I got caught on the table lighters — or the bargain that wasn't!

Once long ago when I was young and green, I owned a small shop which sold cigarettes and gifts. The Ronson salesman called with a really special offer. If we bought their full range of 12 table lighters, Ronson would throw in a thirteenth. Free!

The arithmetic went something like this:

		£
12 lighters: normal cost, say		78.00
Normal selling price (ignoring VAT), say,		120.00
Normal profit margin	35%	42.00
Add selling price of thirteenth free lighter		12.00
Special offer profit margin	45%	£54.00

45 per cent profit sounded good to me. My manager wondered whether he would sell the more expensive lighters, whose retail price ranged from £3 to £25, but he was persuaded by me to take the offer.

We sold two lighters fairly quickly — two of the cheaper ones — and four more over the next nine months. Three years later, we still had three left — not the most expensive but with a retail value of £45. We never did sell them! So instead of making £54, we made £9 and took three years to do it. It was a lousy offer for us — we would have done much better to buy only the three or four lighters we could sell fairly readily and forget the rest.

This is a true story incidentally — though I have adjusted the prices — it happened in the late 1950s! Before Ronson sue me for libel, let me add that there was nothing wrong or unethical about their offer. The products were okay but we were the wrong shop to sell the full range.

Next time someone makes you a special offer if you will buy extra goods, remember:

☐ That you have not earned that lovely fat margin until you have sold the *last* one, not the first. The last one is always the hardest to shift.

☐ That special offers are really nothing special at all unless you know you can sell the extra quantity quickly. Otherwise, given the cost of holding stock, you will do better to buy only what you need now, especially if, as with those lighters, you have to take the full range, not just the quick sellers.

☐ That the manufacturer or wholesaler may be trying to shift slow-moving stock. If he has to offer a special deal, why do you suppose you will sell these lines when others are probably having difficulty in doing so?

There is nothing unethical in the supplier making you a special offer — but make sure it is special for you too, not just for him!

Some points on reducing your stocks

The amount of stock which a business must hold is partly decided by the time it takes to obtain more. Can you reduce the quantities you buy by obtaining more frequent deliveries by suppliers or by using local wholesalers rather than buying direct?

Using cash and carry wholesalers may not be appreciably more expensive when you take into account the costs of holding stock resulting from having to take the minimum orders and to accept the delivery cycles of manufacturers who supply you direct.

If you manufacture yourself, can you shorten your production cycle, thus cutting the stocks you need to hold because you can produce more readily to meet demand? Shortening the cycle often means that stock can be held as raw materials suitable for various products or possibly resaleable as it is, rather than as work in progress or finished goods which are probably useless for any other purpose.

Can you simplify your production so as to use common components for some products?

What is your policy if a customer wants just a few of an item for which your suppliers or considerations of production efficiency dictate larger quantities? Do you charge a premium to cover the surplus stock cost?

Set stock and reorder quantities

Do not leave the amount of stock held and the reorder quantities to the whims of your buyer or stock records clerks. Set figures item by item based upon a policy geared to your delivery times and your plans for new products, budgeted sales etc.

Do you deliver on time?

A British Institute of Management survey in 1978 of 186 manufacturing plants showed that:

> 40 per cent did not formally monitor performance against promised delivery dates.
> 3 per cent had delivered *nothing* on time.
> 20 per cent had delivered 90 per cent of orders on time.
> 3 per cent had delivered everything on time.
> Overall, shop floor production efficiencies were no higher than 30 per cent.

Do you know what your figures are? Much of this appalling inefficiency results from failure to have the right items for each order in the right place when they are needed. A poor delivery record could indicate bad stock control: it certainly means you aren't shifting the stuff through efficiently so your whole system must be clogged up.

Why errors in valuing your stocks can wreak havoc with your figures

Since the stock figure is often so large in relation to others in the balance sheet, errors in pricing it can have a disproportionate effect on the net profit. For example, suppose the true value of your stocks is £100,000 and your correct net profit before tax is £50,000. A 10 per cent over-valuation of your stocks, £10,000, will overstate your net profit by 20 per cent.

The arithmetic gets worse still with a company which is in trouble. Because sales are too low, the quantities of stock are often too high due to difficulties in achieving sales. Over-valuations are both more likely and less easy to spot due to the number of items and the large sums involved. Suppose there is a true loss of £10,000; that same 10 per cent error would eliminate it, so that the business appeared to break even!

The way stock is priced is therefore important. The principle is that it should be valued at the lower of cost or present market value. It's no good putting something in at £100, because that's what you paid for it, if it is obsolete and you can only sell it for £20. So the first point is to be careful when counting stock to note all items which are over-stocked in relation to sales, damaged or whose value is doubtful for some other reason. There's nowt so useless as goods which have been around in your storeroom for a while and which you can't sell in the foreseeable future. The chances are that, if anyone else wants them, they'll only pay a fraction of the normal price. All doubtful items should therefore be written down to realistic figures. More comments on stock values are given on page 127.

Do you make your stock figures tell a story?

Stock-taking is a nuisance but it has to be done. However good your records system is, there will always be differences between the records and what is actually in the stock room. Moreover, many businesses do not have a running record of all items held — you cannot in a small retail shop, for instance, because it is not possible to record each sale.

An annual physical count or, better still, a quarterly one is therefore usually essential. It requires organisation and effort and possibly closing the shop or stopping production. Yet many businesses fail to marshal the resulting information sensibly so as to extract the maximum value from it.

On page 126 is an example of a stock sheet suitable for use in many cases. The sheets should be divided into sections by type of goods, such as raw materials, work in progress and finished goods. Each of these should be subdivided into such headings as type of product or, for production stock such as containers, into bottles, caps, jars, lids, labels etc.

Where the same items repeat, it helps to have master sheets typed with full descriptions which are then photocopied for use at each stock-take. The master can readily be updated for additional lines without having to retype the lot, and the amount of writing needing during the stock count is much reduced: greater accuracy results from fuller and more legible descriptions.

Analyse your stock values by type of stock

When the stock is valued, the value should not be added cumulatively from sheet to sheet. Each should be totalled separately and the total entered on a summary sheet for each heading, such as bottles, caps etc.

That way one can compare not only the *total values* for such categories as raw materials or finished goods from one stock-take to the next but *each sheet*. As you will find you have much the same items on each sheet from one occasion to the next, it becomes easy to spot the variations in value and quantity.

No longer are you looking at just a total of, say, £100,000 but

Example of a stock sheet

Stock sheet for .... Date ....

Type of stock .... Sheet no. ....

1. Is the stock on this page valued at cost (net of VAT) or selling price (including VAT)?
   If at selling price it must be reduced to cost by deducting the average profit margin.
   Check that this margin reduces the price to cost *net of VAT.*
2. Unit of stock means that measure of weight, volume etc. State this if the quantity is not in single units or if there are different sizes of the same item.
3. All calculations of value to be rounded to the nearest £.

Description of item	Unit of stock	Quantity in stock	Price each	Value of stock	Remarks
	Total at cost		£		

at a list broken down into categories and headings. Mistakes in counting or calculating and excessive quantities of stock tend to be highlighted by comparisons with previous counts. The stock figure is often one of the biggest in a balance sheet and is also one of those in which mistakes are most easily made. Organising the stock sheets to permit these comparisons from one count to the next is a great help in getting it right, besides providing a useful guide to where your money is tied up.

The cost figures you use to value your stocks are important

The goods you expect to be able to sell should be valued at cost but this does not necessarily mean the latest price you paid. Be careful not to build in artificial profits in your stock valuation by pricing goods you bought some time ago at the latest manufacturer's increased price. Since raising your stock valuation increases your current profit, you'll pay tax too soon, even if you do sell the goods next year.

Retailers' stock valuations

When valuing stocks, you need good records of the prices you paid if the figures are to be accurate. Many retailers work from selling prices because it is difficult to keep purchase records for large numbers of stock items. Having valued stocks at selling prices, they then take off an average retail margin.

This must be done carefully or it will be inaccurate, also distorting the profit artificially. If you analyse the figures into different kinds of stock or by department, as suggested earlier, it makes it easier to get the figures right because you can use the profit margins applicable to each kind of goods. This is especially important if they vary widely as between, say, cigarettes at 9 per cent and hardware at 30 per cent.

If you use retail prices including VAT, you must use margins which reduce the stock valuation to cost *before* VAT. VAT is not a part of your stock values as you have already recovered it.

Manufacturers' stock valuations

The professional accounting bodies recommend that manufactured stocks and work in progress should be valued to include the overheads incurred in producing them. Be careful if you do this. It is easy to overvalue stocks by including too much overhead.

Never increase the price of individual stock items; always add a percentage on to the total stock value for overheads because otherwise you will not know how much overhead is included in the stock valuation.

If stocks happen to be rather high at your year end and you price every item to include some overhead, it is all too easy to inflate your profit by building in too much overhead. This will not show up in the figures of individual overheads charged in the profit and loss account because they are not affected. It is not the expense totals which are reduced but the stock figure which is increased. The effect is to cut the cost of sales: adding the overhead element as a separate figure in the stock valuation enables you to see its significance and to compare it with your overhead totals.

If you're not sure what I mean by this, try adding £3,400, 10 per cent of the existing value, to the stock figure in the example in Chapter 4 and work out for yourself how the other figures alter. The profit would rise by over 30 per cent because of carrying forward about 9 per cent of the running expenses as the overheads part of the stock valuation.

I use the figures in XYZ shop example because they are in this book. However, only a manufacturer would normally include overheads in the stock valuation, not a retailer or a wholesaler. The idea is that the cost of manufactured goods includes not only the materials and wages needed to produce them but the overheads of the factory as well.

This is a complicated subject and the way the figures are done varies from case to case. However, if overheads are included in your stock valuation, don't let the accountants blind you with science! When they have done the detailed calculations, look yourself at the end result to see if the overhead figure included in the stock valuation makes sense to you. Otherwise you could be storing up trouble by adding in a theoretically sound value for overheads, which doesn't exist in reality.

The 80/20 rule

In any bunch of statistics 80 per cent of the value is likely to be accounted for by 20 per cent of the items. This is true for stocks. If you can identify and give special attention to the 20 per cent of the goods you hold which account for 80 per cent of the value, you will be well on the way to an efficient stock control system.

The converse is that it may not be worth controlling the low value items at all. Nuts, bolts and washers on a production line may be best dealt with on free issue as required since the value is low.

Why have stock records?

☐ To calculate sales and place orders accordingly thus minimising 'out of stocks' in quick selling lines.

☐ To identify slow sellers so that they can be eliminated.

☐ To help plan trading policies based on successful lines.

☐ To help prevent over-ordering or duplicate ordering.

☐ To help locate particular items.

☐ To provide records for accounting and insurance valuation purposes.

☐ In some cases to help price goods.

This is an example of a record card which a retailer might keep. It groups products by manufacturer, rather than by type of item, in order to facilitate ordering.

Example of stock record for retail quick selling lines

Manufacturer's name: CADBURY											
Date	2/1			15/2			2/4			17/5		
Product	Sales	Stock	Order	Sales	Stock	Order	Sales	Stock	Order	Sales	Stock	Order
Milk Choc	15	50	—	20	30	10	20	20	20	15	25	—
Plain Choc	20	15	15	20	10	30	30	10	35	30	15	25
Assortment	30	29	40	44	25	60	65	20	50	35	35	15

This layout gives at a glance the history of a line. Stocks have to cover the period from date of order to arrival of goods so there always have to be some in hand. Stock last time, plus the last order, minus the present stock gives the sales since the last order. As each order comes in, check it off against the record. When each order arrives ring the quantities to show they have been received or amend if necessary to actual quantities received.

How to make up a stock record file for a retailer

This type of record can be kept on the large lever arch files obtainable from most stationers. Make up permanent records for each supplier on pieces of card 1½ inches longer than A4 paper. Write the supplier's name along the top long edge and list his products down the left hand short edge. Punch holes along the top long edge and place on the file. These permanent records do not have to be re-written.

For the stock and order record sheets, use the pads of A4 ruled paper stocked by stationers. Turn the sheets sideways so that the lines run vertically and punch along the top edge but off centre. If you fold so that the left-hand edge is about 4 lines in from the right-hand one, the crease gives the centre for your punch.

Your stock and order record sheets on A4 paper will then be overlapped by the card underneath showing the product names which thus do not have to be rewritten when the sheets are full. All you need do is enter the date on the A4 sheets and head up the columns Sales, Stock, Order as per the previous example. Each sheet will take five such sections comfortably on each side giving you a quick reference to ten orders which is enough for quick selling lines. Since the file is loose leaf, new sheets can be inserted as needed.

When taking stock the cards and sheets can be held on a clip board for ease of handling.

Stock records for slow selling lines and manufacturing stock

Most of your slow selling lines should be of high value (otherwise why sell them?) and may require technical descriptions and other detail.

Similarly a manufacturer's components or materials may be ordered in large quantities which are called off in batches from the supplier, so the records may need to show what is outstanding elsewhere as well as on your premises.

Such items probably require a separate card per item. Complete stock control systems with stationery and binders are made by companies such as Kalamazoo Ltd, Mill Lane, Northfield, Birmingham B31 2RW or Twinlock Ltd, 36 Croydon Road, Beckenham, Kent BR3 4BH. Details can be readily obtained from these companies and are not therefore given here. Many computer systems are now available for small as well as large businesses.

If your business is very small you can get by with your own hand-made stock cards. Properly designed systems save so much time that it is worth having one as soon as you can afford to. See the next heading, however, regarding the difference between stock control and stock recording.

You can only use your stock records to tell you what you have on hand if you are able to update the sales or usage column for each movement. This is usually not practicable for retail fast-moving lines.

The point at which it is no longer safe to rely upon periodic stock-taking is a matter of judgement. To update stock records for every issue or sale can be a slow routine, expensive in time and difficult to keep accurate. Yet a manufacturer, for instance, may need to have such records if only because it is not practicable to check the shelves every time someone wants information on what is available.

The difference between stock recording and stock control

Stock *records* tell you what you have got. A stock *control* system controls what you have got by recording every stock movement as it happens. Under such a system you cannot put stock in or take it out without generating the necessary paperwork.

The objective of a *stock control* system is to minimise your investment in stock while ensuring that you always have what you need and giving you up-to-date figures for stocks held available at any time. Orders for fresh supplies are initiated, or at least suggested, as part of the system.

The difficulty is that such control systems are hard to make work in practice because they demand very high standards both in systems design and in discipline within the organisation. All too easily the stock on paper in the system ceases with the physical reality, whereupon chaos results.

The best stock *control* system is Joe walking round using his eyes — plus accurate forecasts of future sales or usage. *Stock records* are an adjunct to Joe's eyes. So involve your people in stock control. Explain your objectives to them and give them responsibility for helping to keep stocks low.

When your business gets too big for Joe's eyes to keep track, you have to start using your stock records for stock control but keep your system as simple as you can.

Beware of the wild claims made by computer manufacturers that they have a wonderful stock *control* system for you. They may have a good *recording* system which may be worth while if you recognise its role as being limited to helping you to make better decisions by providing more accurate and up-to-date information than can be obtained by hand. Even that is a bold claim in many cases. For instance, suppose your factory or warehouse is at a different location from the computer. Your information will usually be at least a day, possibly two, out of date. The reason is that your despatch details, from which your sales invoices are prepared, and the production figures both have to be taken to the computer before the files can be updated.

That may not matter, or it may mean that the so-called control features of the computer system — such as producing draft production or buying schedules — are useless.

Stock recording is relatively simple, though it does require disciplined paperwork if the figures are to mean much. If you have trouble getting it accurate manually, a computer is unlikely to help. It may make matters far worse because it requires every stock movement to be documented. Even in small organisations, there is often no one person who knows what all the sources of stock movements are so it is not a simple matter to specify the system needs, let alone see whether the computer system meets them.

Stock *control* is not simple. It usually requires a high degree of sophistication and the smaller business normally will do better to rely on managerial decisions based on a good *recording* system. Computer people who do not make this distinction and who try to sell you a control system merely betray their own ignorance of what really matters in management and how a business works. Do not let them blind you to reality in their enthusiasm to sell you a system. The consequences could be dire, and they will not be around to pick up the pieces — not that it would help much if they were.

Summary

Stock eats up cash. Uncontrolled, it will absorb so much money as to prejudice the financing of the business and possibly even to prevent you investing in new activities.

Moreover, cash put into stock is not 'invested'. On the contrary, every £100 of stock can easily cost you £25 in interest charges and wastage. Apart from the financial cost, too much stock will physically inhibit the efficient running of your business.

Keeping stocks low requires:

☐ An understanding of how the business works. Factors such as production or delivery cycles, policy on stock outs and tying purchasing to sales or new product development activity are crucial to decisions on what quantities of stock are needed. The quality of those decisions influences how efficiently stock is matched with the needs of the business.

☐ Sensible systems for recording and counting stock to enable management to know what is happening and to base ordering upon facts rather than guesses.

☐ The careful attention of all employees in implementing the details of the system. If you forget the human factor, it will screw up your stock control and, with it, your production or sales.

☐ A tough attitude to bargain offers.

Pilferage in one form or another will cost you dearly if you do not take precautions. These include physical and paperwork controls. If you want other people to respect your property you must show that you care about it yourself.

Chapter 16

Pricing Your Time

Charging the right price for your time is crucial to your success. Underprice it and, at best, you will work long hours for small reward; at worst your business will fail.

Do you sell time?

Have you thought what it is you really sell? Is it your time or is it goods? Window cleaners and accountants price each job on the time it takes, so they obviously sell their time. However, some businesses which supply goods are really selling time, although this is not always obvious at first sight. If you supply and fit parts, for instance, you probably earn most of your profit from the labour charge, not on the goods supplied. The profit margin on the latter is nowhere near as important as that on the time.

Consider this bill from a vehicle repairer:

	£
Spare parts fitted	100
Labour charge	40
Total	£140

How much profit do you think the invoice might include? We can work it out if we make some assumptions based on typical margins or mark-ups. If you've forgotten the difference between a margin and a mark-up, see Chapter 17.

	Invoice Value £	Profit margin on selling price %	Mark-up on cost %	Cost £	Gross profit £
Spare parts	100	20	25	80.00	20.00
Mechanic's time	40	66⅔	200	13.33	26.67
Totals	£140			£93.33	£46.67

The labour charge contributes substantially more profit even though the charge for parts is two and a half times bigger. And, if the bill was divided equally between parts and labour, ie £70 each, the respective gross profits would be £14 and £46.67 with labour thus contributing 77 per cent of the £60.67 total.

So do not be misled by the value of the parts; the real profit is on the labour. Efficient control of time in the workshop is the key to profitability. The profit on materials supplied is useful but it is small in comparison.

The point applies to many kinds of business. Other examples of people who often supply expensive materials, but who earn most of their profit from the labour involved, are jobbing builders, house painters and anyone who mends things.

Time is also often important to those who make things with their hands. For instance, a producer of arts and crafts is likely to find that much of the cost of each object is the time it takes to make it.

Contrast that with a manufacturer, who uses machinery to make his product. If sales rise, he can produce more to meet demand by running his machines for longer hours or possibly by working them faster. If you are a craftsman working with your hands you have no such flexibility in your supply of time.

If you employ people, as in a repair workshop, you can, of course, expand your sales by taking on more staff. However, people are expensive to recruit and employ and they usually have to be paid whether or not there is work for them. Since each new employee therefore adds substantially to costs, it is vital that the time of the existing ones be properly controlled and correctly priced. Some businesses use outworkers, who operate from home and are paid by the item produced but that is not often practicable.

Is the garage charging an extortionate rate per hour?

In the above example the garage is shown as trebling the cost of the mechanic's time to earn a profit margin of 200 per cent. That may sound exortionate to you but it is not. One reason is that the real cost is much higher than his basic pay per hour, because of all the time, such as holidays, sickness, tea breaks etc for which he is paid but which is not charged to customers. The rate per hour for the time on each job must allow for all these non-chargeable hours.

If you work alone without any employees, you have the same problem. You can never charge out all the time you have. Apart from your own holidays etc there are always administrative jobs to do like the book-keeping, reading official bumf or trade magazines, correspondence or filing, generally organising your day.

If you sell time, you must charge a lot for it

A little further on I explain how to work out how much time you can hope to sell and what to charge for it. But first, here's an important point: Because you've only a limited amount of time, you must charge a lot for it. If your price is too cheap, you'll find yourself working flat out for an inadequate reward. Life is then a vicious circle. You don't make much money nine to five so you work longer hours to improve the score. This has three unpleasant consequences:

1. You have little leisure and you don't see your family as much as you should.
2. You have little time to think, so it is difficult for you to plan the business properly.
3. You still don't earn a really good profit.

All of which is no good to you and is unfair to both your family and your customers. It's unfair to the latter because, if you're harassed and overworked, you'll tend to give them less efficient service; worse, you won't have the time or money to develop your business properly so your customers will suffer in the long run too.

So it's vital to charge enough for your time to give you a decent profit without having to work long hours. Then you have spare capacity either to earn 'super profit' or to develop your business by doing the long-term things which take time to pay off or — most important — to spend some time with your family.

Pricing your own time

Of these three examples which follow, two assume that you are self-employed without staff and therefore selling just your own time. The third applies if you have staff.

Example 1 is a person working freelance from home, such as a labour-only builder or a designer. Example 2 is for someone working from an office, probably with a professional qualification of some kind but still selling only his or her time. Example 3 deals with pricing the time of employees, whose hours you charge out.

The examples start by calculating the *number* of hours you have available. Then they list your expenses so as to arrive at a cost per hour including a basic wage for you. This tells you how much to charge for an hour to earn the minimum you need to live on, assuming reasonable success in selling your services. I suggest you now glance through the first example (on pages 139–40) and then read the following explanatory notes.

How many hours have you available to sell?

Allow for reasonable holidays including bank holidays. These may interrupt the working week by more than one day particularly if you have to work on the premises of your clients. Many businesses shut for an extra day. Some sickness must also be budgeted for.

I suggest at least four weeks' holiday because more and more employees now get this entitlement. If you want to earn a good living in self-employment it is not realistic to budget for shorter holidays whether or not you actually take four weeks in the early years. Indeed, I feel that to compensate for the extra risk and responsibility of being on one's own, five or six weeks holiday is a reasonable allowance.

I take at least six weeks myself, usually more although I do some writing while away! If you decide to plan for more or less than four weeks, alter the number of weeks when doing the costing for your business.

What is a reasonable target to sell?

While a building labourer may be able to sell 100 per cent of his time during a boom, in more normal times neither he nor any other self-employed person can hope to achieve this. The percentage will vary according to the occupation and the work involved to obtain each new assignment. In the building trades a man may well obtain regular work from one or two builders but he is very vulnerable to anything going wrong because he has so few clients. Only you can decide in the circumstances of your business what is a sensible budget for your available time.

If you sell more of your time than the annual total upon which the cost estimate per hour is based you will, of course, make extra profit. Use a conservative estimate of the hours you will sell to allow a safety margin. Do not include overtime in the number of hours upon which you base your costings because you should not have to work long hours to achieve your target. While the number of hours you work may be higher so may your costs. Moreover the target is the minimum that you need to sell in order to earn a living, not what you might like to achieve.

The costs of being in business

The costs figures quoted are only typical figures at the time of writing. You should make your own estimates and work out what kinds of expense you will incur. For instance, you might have machine rental or depreciation costs together with repairs and overhaul of equipment etc. I have put in only a minimal figure for advertising. You could spend this much on entries in two or three Yellow Pages directories alone. Don't underestimate your costs. Build in safety margins to your figures because there are always unexpected items. Costs have a nasty habit of coming out higher than one thought.

Though the working wage is set at £160 a week, you may be quite happy with a lower figure or might require a higher one. The figure used is for you to decide although it is not realistic to use one which is below what you could earn in a job. The 'independence' of working for yourself is often illusory. Most self-employed people are in reality at the beck and call of their customers. One lacks the security of the regular pay packet and the additional stress and responsibility should earn one a higher reward than an ordinary job.

The only exception to this might be a top earning executive who chooses to drop out of a high pressure rat-race type job because he or she wants a more relaxed life style. If that's you, think carefully however. The life style will be different all right but it is unlikely to be relaxed. Working for oneself is hard work and underpricing one's time is a mistake; see Chapter 18.

The pension and life assurance contribution figures used in the examples

A self-employed person can make payments for a personal pension policy which are deductible from his or her earnings for income tax purposes and they also receive favourable tax treatment in the hands of the pension company. The policy can include life assurance cover if desired. These valuable tax concessions mean that a pension policy is a tax efficient way of saving for the self-employed, who are not entitled to the state supplementary pension, only the basic one. As much advantage as possible should be taken of 'retirement annuity relief', as it is called.

The maximum you can pay is 17.5 per cent of your 'net relevant earnings' which are not necessarily the same as net profit. The percentage rises for people over 50.

Since pension provision is an important element of tax planning for the self-employed. I think it should be added to the minimum acceptable weekly profit to calculate the target earnings required. This makes the latter more comparable with the salary you could earn in a job which carries a pension scheme as a fringe benefit.

The figures in the examples are just assumed sums, below the maximum permitted. In Example 1, for instance, a person under 50 could pay 17.5 per cent of the £13,500 total profit, or £2,362.

Technical terms used in the examples

Depreciation is explained in Chapter 4.

Professional fees for a sole trader or a partnership would be mostly the accountants' charges for preparing the annual accounts and agreeing the tax liability with the Inland Revenue. If the business is a limited company, the accountant must issue an 'audit certificate' which involves higher fees as explained in Chapter 2. Apart from accountants' fees, the heading also covers legal costs. In the first year these could be substantial if a business or a property from which to trade has to be bought, a lease negotiated or a partnership agreement prepared.

NI means National Insurance. A self-employed person pays these contributions in two stages. Class 2 are paid either by stamping a card weekly or by authorising the Department of Health and Social Security to make direct debits monthly to your bank account. Class 4 are paid at the same time as your income tax and are calculated on the taxable profit agreed with the tax inspector.

Example 1: A self-employed person without an office

This is an example for someone like a labour-only building sub-contractor, such as a bricklayer, who works on the customer's premises or a person who works from home, perhaps a designer. The figures are hypothetical to show you the principles involved in calculating your own costs. You will not necessarily have the same kind of expenses and the prices will probably have changed anyway by the time you read this so you will have to do your own calculations.

All the costs quoted assume that you are registered for VAT. The first example projects annual sales at below the registration limit. If those were your figures, you would only register voluntarily if you were selling to other registered businesses who could recover the VAT you charged to them. If selling to private customers, it would be better not to register. Non-recoverable VAT would only apply to certain of your costs, rent, for instance, being exempt. To cover the lost VAT, you would not have to raise your prices by as much as the 15 per cent entailed by registration.

The first question is how much time have you got to sell?

	Weeks
Number of weeks in year	52
Less: Own holidays	4
National holidays/sickness (Xmas/New Year 3, Easter 2, May, Spring and Summer) total 8 days + sickness, say 6 days, =	2
Possible working weeks (if no major illness)	46

What percentage of that time can you sell?

85 per cent? Approx 39   weeks × 40 hours = 1560 hours
75 per cent? Approx 34½ weeks × 40 hours = 1380 hours
70 per cent? Approx 32   weeks × 40 hours = 1280 hours
65 per cent? Approx 30   weeks × 40 hours = 1200 hours

Costs of being in business

	£	£
Motor: Insurance and road tax	300	
Repairs and service	500	
Petrol: 240 miles/wk at 30/gal = 8 gals at £1.80 (net of VAT) = £14.40/wk for 46 wks, say	650	
Depreciation: Say 25% of cost of car £6,000:	1,500	
		2,950
Advertising		400
Telephone		400
Insurance — business policies		50
Professional fees		300
Stationery and postage		100
Sundries		300
Total expenses	A	4,500
Profit required net of pension contributions		
Working 'wage', min acceptable say £200/week for 52 wks say		10,400
Pension/life assurance: (see explanation on page 138), say		2,100
Private medical insurance, say		210
NI Class 2; in 1985/86 £3.50/week for 52 wks, say	180	
Class 4; on profit from £4,150 up to £13,780 so £13,780 − £4,150 = £9,630 at 6.3%, say	610	790
Total earnings required (before income tax)	B	£13,500
Total sales required to cover costs and earnings	A + B	£18,000

Which means:

At 85 per cent in 39   weeks £462/week or, for 1,560 hours, £11.54/hr ⎫
At 75 per cent in 34½ weeks £522/week or, for 1,380 hours, £13.04/hr ⎬ plus VAT if
At 70 per cent in 32   weeks £563/week or, for 1,280 hours, £14.06/hr ⎪ applicable
At 65 per cent in 30   weeks £600/week or, for 1,200 hours, £15.00/hr ⎭

Round your hourly rate upwards to, say, £13.10 or £13.20, *not* down to £13.00. Costs are always higher than you think, so build in a safety margin rather than take a chance by trimming your rate.

Example 2: A person working from an office

This person has only his or her time to sell but uses an office and has a part-time secretary/book-keeper. The costs quoted are mostly rather low. If the secretary were full time, the general office expenses would probably be higher as well as her salary. For instance, the depreciation figure I quote here implies, say, £2,000 furniture and fixtures at 10 per cent and £2,500 for equipment such as a typewriter, photocopier etc. This may sound a lot but the total soon mounts up even if you buy second-hand. If you need a computer or word processor, those figures are too low and your stationery costs will also increase.

How much time can be sold?
See the previous example. There are still only 46 weeks in the year.

Costs of being in business		£
Part-time secretary (inc employer's share of NI)		3,450
Motor: As Example 1 but works mostly in office so business mileage less; petrol less and total £2,950 reduces by £350 to		2,600
Rent		2,500
Rates		1,000
Telephone (including answering machine)		1,000
Light and heat		500
Insurance		100
Repairs and maintenance		200
Stationery and postage		200
Professional fees		500
Sundries		950
Depreciation on fixtures, fittings and equipment		700
Total costs	A	£13,700

		£
Profit required net of pension contributions, say		25,000
Pension/life assurance (see earlier explanation), say		5,200
Private medical insurance, say		310
NIC: Class 2; in 1985/86 £3.50/week for 52 weeks, say	180	
Class 4: on profit from £4,150 up to £13,780 so £13,780 − £4,150 = £9,630 at 6.3% say	610	790
Total earnings required	B	£31,300
Total gross fees required	A + B	£45,000

The weekly or hourly rates will be two and a half those in example 1.

Example 3: A repair workshop with ten employees

How many hours can you actually sell?
Suppose your men work a 40-hour five-day week. Each day will include start-up, cleaning and close down periods, tea breaks, waiting time, stores issue queues etc. The exact nature of these depends upon the business but you are bound to lose some of the day in time which cannot be charged to customers.

You may find you can only expect 80 per cent of the day to be actually spent on the job, in which case, of your available hours $46 \times 40 = 1,840$, you can sell 80 per cent = 1,472 hours per man.

What is your direct cost per employee?
The figures given illustrate some typical items making up the direct cost of employing staff. You may well have different items in your business but the principles will be the same.

Number of available working weeks: 46 weeks as for previous examples	
Assuming 40 hour 5-day week, each man is present for	1840 hours
If he does chargeable work for 80 per cent of the time, you can sell	1472 hours
What are your direct costs per employee?	£
Suppose the average basic weekly wage of your people is	150.00
To this you must add the cost to the employer of various items	
Employer's National Insurance (10.45% in 1985/86)	15.68
Canteen/luncheon voucher/subsistence allowances, say	4.00
Protective clothing and tools, say	1.32
Direct cost per employee Weekly	£171.00
× 52 = annual cost each	£8,892.00
Calculating a rate/hour to include overheads	£
Suppose you have 10 men whose annual cost is therefore	88,920
Suppose your overheads are similar to those in Example 2 but higher as this is a larger business. Let's also allow for a full-time receptionist/secretary/book-keeper/general assistant, who is not charged out to each job, so we'll increase the £13,700 to, say	28,820
Add interest on loan or bank overdraft (or, if you owe nothing, a return on the money you put in yourself to finance the business), say	1,300
Add your own minimum earnings target — as per Example 1	13,500
Minimum turnover required	£132,000
which for 1,472 × 10 = 14,720 hours saleable = approx	£8.97/hr

But this does not allow for any 'super profit' or reward for the risk and responsibility of having your own business.

	£
Suppose you want a super profit of another £10,500: to earn that over 14,720 hours, you must add approx	0.71
	£9.68/hr
So you would round your labour rate to	£9.70/hr

You must work out your own rates per hour

Do not use the rates per hour in my examples. Work out your own after deciding:

☐ How much time you can sell.
☐ Whether the costs are realistic in your case.

Any variation in either of these factors could make a big difference to the rate per hour. For instance, any travel time to reach customers, which you cannot charge to them, has to come out of the allowance for unsold time, which you make when you assume you will sell 75 per cent, 70 per cent or whatever of your available hours.

And what will be *your* annual mileage in your car?. Many people do far more than 10,000 miles a year on business.

Although the time sold is expressed in terms of weeks, this is the same thing as saying that, if you sell some time in *each* of the 46 available weeks, you will achieve an average per week of 34½ hours charged out if you sell 75 per cent, about 32 hours if you sell 70 per cent and so on.

What factors could alter the total cost per hour?

The £9.70 hourly rate depends upon the following factors:

☐ Proportion of chargeable time actually charged out.
☐ Number of people employed on chargeable work.
☐ Changes in wage costs.
☐ Changes in fixed costs.

A key assumption in the calculation of the hourly rate in Example 3 is that 80 per cent of the men's time during the 46 working weeks will be sold. Any variation from this will affect the cost.

If you do chargeable work yourself for some of the time, an estimate of that part of your time should be added to the figure for saleable hours. A similar proportion of your salary can then be included in direct costs.

When working out your own figures, try seeing how much the

143

answer alters when you change an assumption about one of these factors. That will show you how sensitive your calculations are to errors in your estimates.

How much 'super profit' should I aim for?

In deciding how much 'super profit' to aim for, take into account how risky the business is — more people go bust in the building trade than in most others for instance — and how much capital you have tied up in it which would earn you interest if it were in the bank.

Don't be swayed too much by your competitors' prices. Many businesses bankrupt themselves trying to undercut the rest. Price is only one factor in a customer's decision as to who he buys from. Quality, reliability and getting the job done on time are often just as important to him. For more on this point, see Chapter 18.

Poor control of time will destroy your profitability

Taking the figures calculated in Example 1, to budget for 70 per cent of time sold gives a rate per hour of £14.06 for 1,280 hours. But if you achieve only 65 per cent of time sold — 1,200 hours — you have lost 80 hours at £14.06 = £1,125. On planned sales of £18,000, that makes a hole of about 6.3 per cent.

Another way of looking at it is that you ought to have charged £15.00 per hour, the rate corresponding to 65 per cent efficiency.

If you budget for 65 per cent at £15.00 and achieve 70 per cent, you gain 80 hours at £15.00 = £1,200, which raises your sales by 6.7 per cent to £19,200.

These losses or profits may seem marginal but remember that they are at the top end of what you earn so their true significance is their impact on your net spending money.

Suppose you need £13,500 minimum but budget to earn £17,000 so as to gain a 'super profit' or true reward of £3,500 in return for the risk and responsibility of your own business. Your budgeted sales in Example 1 would have to be £21,500. A £1,000 shortfall due to not controlling your time properly is only 4.7 per cent of that £21,500 but it cuts the real reward of £3,300 by nearly 30 per cent!

Don't treat your costings as inviolate

The labour rates produced by all these calculations should not be interpreted rigidly as meaning that work is unacceptable at a lower figure. They are a guide, a basis for making a judgement only. If you need work but can only get it at £10 per hour, you may have to take it at that rate. Some income is better than none. The decision should be based upon your position at that time. If you obtain work substantially above your hoped for average rate next time, you may still reach your target for the year.

Thus your pricing policy must be flexible. Perhaps work at £20 per hour can be obtained at certain times of the year, while jobs have to be accepted at £10 at other times.

Materials

Materials are omitted from these calculations because profit is not normally earned upon them. They are part of the costs of the job to be added to your price for your labour.

If you do not make a profit on, say, spare parts, you should estimate the cost of what you use during the year. You can then easily calculate the contribution to your profits by applying your normal mark-up to that total. This gives you the amount of the margin you will earn. Since there will be costs — even if you hold no stocks there are bound to be some expenses to eat into that margin — it is best to regard it as an addition to the profit you make selling your time rather than enabling you to reduce the amount you need to charge for that time.

Costing records

Costing records for each job are vital to controlling your business. Whether or not you show labour charges separately from materials on your invoices, you should have a breakdown in your job records. These should show, job by job, the materials or parts used on it and the time spent on it. Then you can compare the actual results of particular jobs with the costings of them. This is an essential discipline. It shows you where you make or lose money and provides valuable information upon which to plan your business.

Finally a cautionary tale about pricing too low as told to the *Financial Times*.

A young veterinary surgeon, eager to make a name for himself and therefore happy to turn out at all hours, drove out to an isolated farm one night in answer to an 'emergency' call. Arriving at the holding and asking to be led to the ailing beast, he was told there was no veterinary crisis.

'I have to get into town in a hurry,' the farmer said. 'My car's broken down and your visiting fee is less than the mini-cab fare.'

If you charge too little, people will abuse your time too!

Questions

☐ What are your own figures for:
  (a) Time available?
  (b) Expected proportion of time sold?
  (c) Costs?
☐ Using the principles explained in this chapter, what should be your rate per hour?

Chapter 17

Pricing Your Product

The previous chapter dealt with how to arrive at the price per hour to charge for your time. This one explains how to fix a price for a product you make.

There are two ways to approach the problem:

What does it cost me to make? *Or*
What is the most the customer will pay me for it?

It is very important to charge as much as the market will bear. Underpricing can mean a business fails. The next chapter discusses why.

However, most people have to begin by working out what the product will cost to produce; if only because if it is a new idea, it may be difficult to know what people will pay for it.

The trouble with the question, 'How much does it cost to make?' is that there is no one answer. It depends on various factors. For example, it usually gets cheaper the more you produce so you need to know how many.

Then it also depends on which expenses you regard as part of the cost of production and which are just general overheads.

In theory one can divide costs into direct ones which vary more or less in ratio with the quantity produced, and fixed costs which stay much the same, whether you make a few or a lot.

The materials used in the product are an obvious direct cost. The rent of the factory is a fixed cost — until the next rent review, anyway.

Sadly, life is not so simple. Take materials. They do not vary directly! Why not? The reasons differ according to the business. In a factory, the wastage in warming up or changing over machines tends to be similar, whether it is a short or a long run, so longer runs reduce the waste per unit. With long runs, production workers become more practised thus reducing wastage too and output is higher because less time is taken up in changing from product to product on the machines.

In a small business, purchase prices for materials tend to be high because the orders placed with suppliers are small. Moreover, if you have to place orders of a minimum size, small sales mean left-over quantities of material or part-made goods lying about your premises which usually deteriorate or perhaps become unusable because of changes in demand. This is a big risk in a fashion business, for instance. Increase the throughput and you buy cheaper while reducing your wastage.

So the problem often is that one cannot work out the *direct* cost per unit without first deciding the quantity one expects to sell. As for the *fixed* costs, they obviously vary even more according to the quantity. For example, if your fixed costs are £20,000 a year for rent, rates, telephone, depreciation etc, the amount per unit for a sale of 20,000 units is £1 but double that if you think you will shift only 10,000 units.

How marginal costing can help you

Marginal costing sounds like a horrible piece of accounting jargon but its meaning is simple and very important. Variable costs alter with sales volume. Fixed costs do not. An order at a price which covers all variable costs and contributes something towards fixed costs may be worth having even though the price is low.

A department or product may be worth keeping even though it apparently does not cover its fixed costs. Marginal costing seeks to identify such situations.

How a potter could profit from a big order at a low price

The potter makes mugs. His costs are as follows:

	£
Rent and rates	3,000
Electricity	1,500
Motor expenses	1,000
Telephone, stationery etc	500
	£6,000

For practical purposes these costs do not alter however many mugs he makes. Of course his electricity bill will increase as he uses his equipment more but the alteration in cost of electricity per mug will not be significant over a range of production volumes.

Suppose his cost of materials per mug is 40p and his average sales are 213 mugs per week in the 47 weeks available to him annually: say 10,000 mugs a year. His fixed costs of £6,000 pa are thus 60p per mug. With materials his total cost per mug is £1.00. If he sells at £1.60 each he has a profit of 60p each or £6,000 pa.

Marginal cost of the potter
His marginal cost is 40p per pot: ie the cost for materials per pot which changes directly according to the number he makes.

Can the potter take a big order at a low price?
A customer offers him an order for 4,000 mugs but at £1.30 only. He can make the mugs without prejudicing other sales but his total cost of £1 per mug leaves him a profit per unit halved to 30p on this order. Is this correct thinking? How does he decide whether or not to take the order?

New fixed cost per mug
If, for the same fixed costs of £6,000, he now makes 14,000 mugs, his fixed cost per mug is 42.9p — say 43p.

New profit calculation
The position then is:

	£
He sells 10,000 mugs @ £1.60	16,000
He sells 4,000 mugs @ £1.30	5,200
Total sales 14,000	21,200
Less: variable cost of materials	
14,000 @ 40p	5,600
Fixed costs	6,000
Net profit	£9,600

Why is net profit up by nearly 50 per cent from £6,000 to £9,600?
His extra profit is made up thus:

	£
4,000 mugs sold at profit of 47p (£1.30 – 40p – 43p)	1,880
10,000 mugs sold at profit of 77p (£1.60 – 40p – 43p)	7,700
Differences due to rounding up cost to 43p	20
Net profit: 68.6p per mug on average	£9,600

Thus he made less profit per mug on the big order but the increased production meant that his fixed costs per mug were 60p – 43p = 17p lower. His overall profit per mug was thus 8.6p higher even though he took the big order at a cut price.

High volume equals low fixed costs

In fact the potter could make more money by taking an order at any price which covered his materials cost and made some contribution towards his fixed costs. If you are in a similar position, don't take my example too literally, however. I have over-simplified the kind of situation usually found in business. For one thing fixed costs tend to increase a little with higher volume. You can't run machines for extra hours without eventually increasing the repair bills, for instance. Then if you set too low a price for a volume order, it may make it more difficult for your other customers to sell and thus reduce your sales to them.

Also if you cut prices too far, you could find you end up working harder to produce more goods at lower profits per item and that, after paying your fixed costs, you make no more profit!

Another danger is that you increase *your* sales volume to a point at which you cannot meet your orders without extending your facilities thus increasing your fixed costs and making some of your lower priced deals unprofitable. More about this later.

Nevertheless, the principle is that high volume reduces fixed costs per unit and often makes for higher profits in spite of lower prices. This may seem to conflict with the idea that you must charge the highest price you can get which is explained in the next setion. The point is that, when fixing your ordinary price, you must set it high. Then, if someone offers you a big order, you can do the arithmetic to see whether it is worth taking at the price offered.

Another point about pricing a product or service

If your product or service has a high variable cost, a price increase may raise profits in spite of lower volume sales. The reverse applies if the variable cost is low. Thus:

Product or service	Before A	Before B		After A	After B
Sales 100 units at £1	£100	£100			
Raise prices by 10%:					
Volume falls by 15%					
so 85% = £150				£93.50	£93.50
Variable cost 60% for A	£60		85 at 60p	£51.00	
30% for B		£30	85 at 30p		£25.50
Contribution	£40	£70		£42.50	£68.00

Thus for a 10 per cent price rise and a 15 per cent sales fall the contribution goes up for the product with the high variable cost/low contribution but down for the one with the low variable cost/high contribution. Now calculate the effect of a price reduction of 10 per cent. What increase in volume is needed to earn the same contribution that each product earns at £1?

	A	B
Selling price is now	90p	90p
Contribution per unit is 40p – 10p	30p	
70p – 10p		60p
Total contribution wanted to maintain profits	£40	£70
No of unit sales required (£40 ÷ 30p: £70 ÷ 60p)	113	117
An increase of	33.3%	17%

Thus you need to understand the relationship of prices, costs and sales volumes for your products or services if you are to make the best decisions on how much to charge. Beware of distorting the facts by the arbitrary division of costs. Let's see what that means.

A more complicated costing situation with three products

Suppose you have three products. You analyse your accounts to show the following position:

		Total		A		B		C
	%	£	%	£	%	£	%	£
Sales		100,000		60,000		30,000		10,000
Gross profit (contribution to fixed costs)	15	15,000	10	6,000	20	6,000	30	3,000
Fixed costs (divided in proportion to sales)	12	12,000	12	7,200	12	3,600	12	1,200
Net profit (Loss)	3	£3,000	(2)	(£1,200)	8	£2,400	18	£1,800

Net profit is poor. What action do you take? Do you cut out product A because it appears to make a loss?

Cut out product A
Suppose you promote product C hard because of its high gross profit. You double its sales and stop selling product A. The position is then:

		Total		B		C
	%	£	%	£	%	£
Sales		50,000		30,000		20,000
Gross profit (contribution to fixed costs)	24	12,000	20	6,000	30	6,000
Fixed costs (in proportion to sales)	24	12,000	24	7,200	24	4,800
		Nil	(4)	(£1,200)	6	£1,200

Where has all the profit gone?
You cut out a loss-making product. You pushed hard the one making

151

the highest profit and doubled its sales. This decisive action has resulted in your losing what little profit you had. Why?

Do not allocate costs arbitrarily

The answer lies in the fixed costs. The gross profit is a contribution to those costs. Product A contributed £6,000 towards them. The loss of £1,200 on product A was a notional one only. Such nonsense figures result from the obsession of accountants with allocating costs which should not be allocated. There was no logical basis for splitting the fixed costs in proportion to sales. It was convenient but it had no relevance to the business situation.

The real position was a total contribution by the three products of £15,000 towards the fixed costs of £12,000. Cutting out product A did not reduce the fixed costs. Since the increased contribution by product C from its extra sales was only £3,000 the loss of £6,000 from product A eliminated the net profit. The real problem was not the theoretical 'loss' made on A but how to increase the total gross profit or contribution towards fixed costs and profit made by all three products.

Limitations upon marginal costing

Marginal costing is a useful technique. Like all techniques it must not be misused. Business decisions are not usually as simple as in the above examples but the idea that one should not arbitrarily apportion fixed costs is an important one. The key is to maximise the *contribution* made by your products towards your fixed costs and profit. So long as a product makes a contribution, it should be retained until you reach your sales capacity. At that point, it may pay to drop it to make room for a more profitable one rather than invest in expanding your capacity.

Again, the example above is over-simplified to make the point. The gross profit on a product is only the same as the contribution it makes if there are no other costs of selling, distribution etc which relate to it specifically. For instance, some products may be more expensive to sell. Your measurements of contribution should take account of such differences.

Will you need extra investment if you take that big order?

Big orders at low prices often mean that extra equipment to increase capacity has to be bought, thus raising costs. If you raise your unit sales higher than your factory can produce, by accepting extra business at low prices, you may find that what was profitable when you had spare capacity now loses you money. The reason will be that your fixed costs have gone up because of the need to increase capacity by buying new machines or extending the factory and that the margin on those extra orders does not cover the increase in fixed costs required to service them.

When you reach your production capacity consider restricting sales at low prices or cutting out less profitable products. Do not automatically take on extra business at cut prices. Consider the whole picture.

Maximising profit is the aim

The object is to maximise profit, not sales. If your shop or factory is overstretched, it may pay you to cut out your least profitable activities but only if you have correctly measured the variable costs (marginal cost) relating to them.

Sometimes an unprofitable product or activity is a 'loss leader' which brings in other good business and has to be retained for that reason.

Beware of high margin lines

To maximise profit it is tempting to push the high margin lines which show the greatest contribution. But this can be a false trail. High margins often go with low volume. Better profits may result from promoting lines with average margins but volume sales potential.

Questions

☐ What is the principle of marginal costing? Check your answer with the text.

☐ You make wooden crates. The cost of materials used for each crate is £2 and the direct labour costs you £3 in wages. Last year's sales were 50,000 crates. Your overhead costs, including your own pay, were £75,000.

(a) What was your total cost per crate? Marginal cost per crate?

(b) A new customer offers you an order for 10,000 crates at £6.00.

Do you take it?

What points do you consider when deciding?

153

(c) You find that you can only handle the business if you increase your overhead costs by £15,000 pa. Do you take the
order?

☐ You have three products. Their selling prices and other figures
are as follows:

Product	A	B	C
Selling price	£1	£4	£6
Gross margin (%)	20%	30%	15%
Quantity sold	8,000	3,000	3,000
Total floor space 1,000 sq ft			
Floor space occupied (%)	25%	35%	40%
Stocks held (based on cost, remember)	8 weeks	12 weeks	3 weeks

1. What is the proportion of total sales which each product
produces?
What is the proportion of the total gross margin which each
product contributes?
What are the sales per square foot for each product?
What is the gross profit per square foot for each product?
What is the stock value for each product?
What is the order of profitability of the products based on:
☐ Space usage?
☐ Investment in stock?

2. If your space were limited, which product would you cut down
on and which would you promote?
If you were short of cash, to which product would you give
most attention and which would you promote?

Answers

(a) Total cost per crate   £6.50
    Marginal cost per crate   £5.00
(b) You take the order provided that you can handle it within
    your existing capacity without increasing your costs.
    You consider the possible effects on the market price for your
    crates if others hear of the low price and you look carefully
    for any extra cost involved. On the other hand, you look for
    possible reductions in materials and direct labour per crate
    resulting from 20 per cent higher throughput.
(c) You do not take the order if you will have to increase your
    overheads by £6,000. The order would contribute £1 per crate
    or £10,000 towards overheads so you would lose £5,000.

Question 1
All percentages to nearest whole.

	Total	A	B	C
Product sales	£38,000	£8,000	£12,000	£18,000
Proportion of sales	100%	21%	32%	47%
Cost of sales	£30,100	£6,400	£8,400	£15,300
Gross profit	21% £7,900	20% £1,600	30% £3,600	15% £2,700
Gross profit contributed (%)	100%	20%	46%	34%
Floor space occupied (%)	100%	25%	35%	40%
Floor area used in sq ft	1,000	250	350	400
Sales per sq ft	£38	£32	£34	45
Gross profit per sq ft	£7.90	£6.40	£10.30	£6.75
Stock value (based on cost of sales)	6.6 £3,800	8 £980	12 £1,940	3 £880
	52	52	52	52

Note how misleading the sales and gross profit percentages are as a guide to true profitability. Gross profit per square foot shows quite a different order of merit from sales per square foot. Note also how the totals conceal wide variations between the products.

Product B earns most gross profit per square foot and so would be promoted, with product C taking second place if space was short.

Product C requires the least investment in stock. It is a low margin, fast moving line of high unit value — such as cigarettes. Product B is a high margin line requiring stocks to service sales. A cash shortage could be helped by a careful review of the stocks held for product B. As B is the largest investment in stock, a small improvement will have the greatest effect.

The danger of reducing stocks of B is that sales might suffer. This could be serious because of the very high gross profit per square foot of space. However, customers might accept some element of waiting time — this is probably not a product bought on impulse.

Let's see how the figures might work out:

Suppose the stocks of B can be cut by 10 per cent. This releases cash of	£194
It also releases floor space of 35 sq ft. Suppose this space can be used for a new line at the same profit margin as C.	
Assume that stocks of the new line in the same proportion of stocks to floor area as C so new stock absorbs thus: £880 ÷ 400 sq ft = £2.2 × 35 sq ft	£77
Net cash released from stocks	£117

If sales of B fall by 5 per cent as a result of reduced stocks

Reduction is £600 @ gross profit of 30 per cent	£180
Suppose the stocks of new product represent 3 weeks usage as for C	
Usage is then 77 ÷ 3 × 52 = £1,335	
Grossed up the usage for a gross profit of 15 per cent, suggests sales of £1,570 and gross profit of:	£235
Gross profit increase	£55

This exercise shows you how, given some simple assumptions, you can work out the financial results of changing the way the business works. It is of course a theoretical example based on simple suppositions and using small figures, but it demonstrates the scope for profit improvement by management able to use financial information properly.

Never, however, make decisions based on figures alone. All figures are based on assumptions and assumptions are often either guesses or crude estimates. Always check with the people affected by the new policy to see if there are reasons why either the assumptions are inaccurate or why the theory won't work in practice.

Chapter 18

Why You Ought to Charge a Lot for What You Do

In the previous two chapters I have shown you how to arrive at the *minimum* price you can afford to sell at. Now here's some more about the importance of charging the *highest* price you can get.

Most businesses have some choice over their prices

There are more businesses which have a choice between charging a high or a low price than you might think. Although wholesalers and retailers mostly cannot charge more than the manufacturer's suggested prices and often have to discount them, even they have a choice of *how much* discount to offer.

An example of a trade with no fixed prices is cosmetics. Although pots of face cream tend to cost much the same to make, they sell for widely differing prices depending upon the marketing policy and image of the manufacturer. This being a dreams and illusions market, each maker must decide how he wishes to position himself in the public eye. The image options range from good value, no frills preparations to super luxury, top priced exclusivity. Only at the bottom end does price top the list of consumer reasons for purchase, if indeed it does then. The more expensive brands must first establish an image of quality, reliability and style as selling points and heavy marketing expenditure is necessary to do this. Prices are, of course, influenced by the competition in the particular section of the market in which the manufacturer wishes to compete but they are not the key selling point.

As a contrast, take a baked beans manufacturer who sells a product roughly the same as anyone else's. In theory he cannot deviate much from the usual price per can. In practice, even he has some scope for improving his prices by careful negotiation to restrict the discounts for quantity, which the big retailers demand from him.

Another type of market is for a technical product which sells on performance. A factory machine or an office photocopier, for instance, probably has several apparent competitors. However, these are likely to vary considerably in their precise capabilities, mode of operation etc, and the customer's buying decision is often based on these points with the price a secondary consideration (within limits, naturally). And, of course, a new product may have no directly comparable competition at all. The first desk calculators, for instance, gave business executives a new tool. Previously the only means of doing one-off calculations were slide rules, which were slow, and comptometers, which required trained operators.

Some types of service are highly price competitive but many others are not as much as they appear to be. A launderette or a window cleaner may in theory be constrained by the prices others charge, but even they can justify and obtain more than average if they offer a better service.

In many cases, particularly when the customer is another business, it is quality and speed of service which come before price.

Get the best price you can

Fixing your prices is one of the most important business decisions you'll make! If you have a choice you must charge the highest price you can get. To see why, let's take the example of a new product you've developed for which there is no competition at the moment — or at least nothing directly comparable.

Suppose it is not an exclusive luxury product and you therefore hope to get volume sales. Indeed you probably need to in order to make a profit at the low price which would make the product easy to sell.

The temptation is to pitch the initial price low. That's usually a mistake. If you can spend a lot of money on advertising and promotion, you may get the volume you need. If not you're probably only going to sell a few at first no matter how low the price. Why? Because no one knows you, no one knows your product. It's a new idea and people need time to accept new ideas.

If you sell direct, you will have to keep repeating your advertising and your mail shots or salesmen's visits to prospective customers. You will need sales literature and must pay either heavy postage costs for mailing shots to prospects or provide them, together with sales aids such as samples or mock-ups, to your salesmen. The latter will want cars if they are full time. Even if you use part-time agents, they need supporting and administering.

If you sell through retailers it won't be easy or quick getting them to stock and display your wondrous idea, let alone explain it properly to prospective buyers.

One way or another, it will take you time and cost you a bomb to get the message to your potential customers. Sales will be slower than you hoped and will cost more to get than you budgeted for. Charging a high price may help to sell the idea by giving it an exclusive image. It will allow you to give a better commission to those who sell for you, whether salesmen or retailers, thus making it more rewarding for them. And the higher margin per unit will usually give you more profit out of which to finance your marketing. Remember you are unlikely to sell a lot whatever you do. Runaway successes in new ideas are few. Most take time and hard graft to get established so a good profit on the sales you do achieve is vital.

If I sound over-pessimistic about your chances, remember that the above has been the story of many good ideas. The failure rate is high and even those which survive often do not produce anywhere near the hoped-for rewards to their originators because they are marketed too cheaply. High prices will enable you to pay for the marketing expenses necessary to sell the product or service. They provide a cushion to cope with the inevitable unforeseen costs. Once sales start to build up, they provide the cash necessary to plough back to improve the product, develop the market and to finance expansion.

Resist the temptation to set the lowest price you can for fear of the customer. Price up and then use the additional profit to market aggressively, to show off and publicise your product or service. If it is any good and you have allowed yourself enough cash for marketing, you'll find enough selling points to attract buyers.

You are never going to sell to every potential purchase anyway. Many sales will be stymied by reasons outside your control such as established connections elsewhere, wrong person approached, too much of another product in stock, or he's just feeling like saying 'no'; umpteen are the reasons why your sales approach will fail in a proportion of cases whatever you do. Of course, you will overcome many of them, either by persistence or by correcting your own mistakes, but this costs money and takes time.

Your price will always be too high for some people no matter how low you set it. Forget them. Set a figure to give you a really good margin. If your product or service and your marketing approach are adequate you will find enough customers to more than pay for the ones you lose on price.

Once you've got going, the initial high price enables you either to make cuts as your competitors catch up and copy you, or to finance the research necessary to stay one jump ahead technically.

An example of the arithmetic of high prices

Direct variable cost per unit of your product (cost of sales)	£5
Other costs which do not vary directly with each unit (selling, advertising, administration etc)	£30,000

How many units must be sold to cover fixed costs if price is £10?
Answer. Fixed costs must be met from margin after paying variable costs.
So £30,000 divided by the gross profit (£10 – £5) = £5; so breakeven is   **6,000 units**

	£
say 6,000 units sell at £10	60,000
Cost of sales at £5 each × 6,000 = direct costs	30,000
Break-even point: gross profit equals the other costs	30,000

Suppose that you could have obtained £12 per unit without loss of sales. The arithmetic is then:

6,000 units at £12	72,000
Cost of sales at £5	30,000
Other costs	30,000
Profit	£12,000

Or, looking at it another way, the break-even point is now £30,000 divided by £7 (the new gross margin) = 4,286 units, a considerable reduction from 6,000.

Now let's compare the results over the next three years for the two prices assuming:

(a)   Selling prices stay the same at £10 and £12.
(b)   Initial sales 8,000 units.
(c)   Growth in sales of 25 per cent per year.
(d)   Variable costs stay the same, the cost per unit being held down by the rising number of units sold.
(e)   Other costs rise by 10 per cent.
(f)   You take out a salary of £10,000, then £11,000 then £13,000.

Year	Sales Prices		Sales units	Gross margin at £5	at £7	Fixed costs	Salary	Net profit	
	A	B		A	B			A	B
	£	£		£	£	£	£	£	£
1	10	12	8,000	40,000	56,000	30,000	10,000	Nil	16,000
2	10	12	10,000	50,000	70,000	33,000	11,000	6,000	26,000
3	10	12	12,500	62,500	87,500	36,300	13,000	13,200	38,200
						Total profit		£19,200	£80,200

Startled by the arithmetic? A 20 per cent increase in price more than quadruples the net profit earned over three years! At or near break-even point, a price increase has a dramatic effect on profits, as you can see. The arithmetical ratio of the higher profits to the lower ones then decreases each year but this is misleading. The extra profit rises from £16,000 to £20,000, then £25,000.

Why is it so important to earn good profits?

The answer has nothing to do with politics or the fair distribution of wealth. Such considerations only start to apply when high *disposable* profits are earned. Usually with a new company or a new product, the extra profit is not disposable; it is badly needed to pay back money borrowed for the project, to finance expansion or to provide the extra working capital needed for the growing level of sales.

Let's calculate the working capital needed to finance a manufacturer on the basis of the figures in this example. We'll assume that Debtors (accounts receivable) and Stocks of materials and finished goods each represent six weeks' sales and that Creditors (accounts payable) allow four weeks' credit for purchases. To keep it simple, we'll ignore VAT which, if applicable to sales, increases the Debtors balances and is payable on many purchase and expense invoices, thus inflating Creditors too.

At £10 and £12 per unit, sales in year 3 will be £125,000 and £150,000. Assuming that sales rise steadily throughout the period, weekly turnover might be £2,750 and £3,300 (both 275 units) at the end of the third year.

The working capital needed by the end of year 3 will then be as follows:

	Low price £	High price £
Debtors will be the final six weeks' sales	16,500	19,800
Stocks at cost (275 units × 6 × £5 for both)	8,250	8,250
	24,750	28,050
Less financed by creditors: four weeks' purchases (275 units × 4 × £5 plus, say, £1,500 fixed costs)	5,500	5,500
Working capital required by end of year 3:	£19,250	£22,550

Comparing these figures with the net profits calculated above shows that the low price will not generate enough cash to finance the business. The working capital figure does not include anything for expenditure on fixed assets, such as equipment or premises, while the profits shown earlier are before paying tax. On the other hand, the high price will handsomely cover the immediate needs leaving a balance to invest in the future by buying new equipment, launching a bigger marketing campaign or whatever.

I have shown you a simplified version of real life, in order to make the key points clear.

If your product is new and without competition, it is only a matter of time before someone else copies you. You need profits to pay for research on technical improvements to keep you ahead. A high starting price may, of course, stimulate competition but it also gives you the scope to reduce your prices when the newcomers undercut you: by then you will be established while they will still be learning the ropes with all the attendant start-up costs and they will not find it easy to retaliate.

The extra profit makes all the difference to the company

To summarise, set your prices as high as you dare. In many situations a better price can be obtained for the sacrifice of relatively few sales. Remember it is easier to reduce prices than to increase them.

The extra profit obtainable from correctly pricing a product or service is likely to make all the difference to the future of the business. It provides self-generated cash to finance expansion, further development of the product or to pay for new facilities. It may enable you to avoid further borrowings, which are difficult and expensive to obtain for a young company, and to pay back existing loans.

For the owners it means that the existing owners stay in charge because they can continue to finance development. They are not forced to sell out to a larger organisation or to restrict growth.

For the employees it means a larger cake out of which can come the money for better working conditions and the investment in new plant, more research etc which will keep the company in business a few years hence, ie, good profits mean job security. Only when there is money to meet all the future needs of the business is the surplus truly disposable. Then it may be a matter of politics or social justice that some of it be distributed elsewhere than the owner's pocket. Until you reach that happy position, high prices are essential to your business survival, not just a rip-off!

Part 3
Basic Figures

Chapter 19

Simple Business Calculations

Some people have difficulty with business arithmetic. This chapter explains a few calculations which may cause problems.

Percentages

To find what percentage 40 is of 320 divide thus:

$$\frac{40}{320} = 0.125$$

Move the decimal point two places right and you have the percentage, ie 12½% (per cent). Prove this to yourself thus:

10 on 100 is 10%: $\quad \frac{10}{100} = .10 = 10\%$.

Profit mark-up

Mark-up is the percentage profit based on cost.

Profit margin

Margin is the percentage profit based on selling price.

Comparison of mark-up and margin

The same sum of profit is a lower percentage when expressed as a profit margin than it is when calculated as a profit mark-up. Some examples are given in the table below on page 166.

Many people confuse both themselves and others by not being clear whether they are quoting a mark-up or a margin. 100 per cent has to be a mark-up, because one cannot have a sale price which is all profit. 25 per cent could easily be either, and you should make sure which is meant.

Cost £	Profit £	Selling price £	Mark-up	Fraction	Margin	Fraction
100	100	200	100%	1	50%	$\frac{1}{2}$
100	50	150	50%	$\frac{1}{2}$	33.3%	$\frac{1}{3}$
100	25	125	25%	$\frac{1}{4}$	20%	$\frac{1}{5}$
100	80	180	80%	$\frac{4}{5}$	44.4%	$\frac{4}{9}$

Note that a mark-up fraction can be converted to a margin fraction by adding the numerator (top half) to the denominator (bottom half). The top half stays the same. Thus a mark-up of $\frac{1}{2}$ is a margin of $\frac{1}{3}$, $\frac{4}{5}$ becomes $\frac{4}{9}$ and so on.

Which to use — mark-up or margin?

When pricing individual articles, you use mark-up because you know the cost and you are calculating the selling price.

When discussing the average gross profit you obtain overall, however, it is better to think in margin terms. You know your total sales — what is in the till or on your invoices. You do not usually know your total cost of goods sold without drawing up accounts. So in calculating total profits it is easier to work out margin on sales than mark-up on cost.

In pricing individual products, use cost and calculate mark-ups. Once you have decided your policy on either mark-up or margin, the other ratio follows. Naturally an average mark-up of 50 per cent will not produce an actual margin of 33⅓ per cent because of stock losses of various kinds.

For example, a retail boutique may mark up at 100 per cent: ie a margin of 50 per cent. But it will probably not achieve an actual margin much above 35 to 40 per cent, depending on how skilfully the owner buys. There is always unsold stock to be cleared at reduced prices, plus pilferage etc, which cuts the actual margin obtained.

Eliminate VAT (value added tax)

If VAT applies, it must be taken out of both cost and sales prices to get the true profit margin. If all your sales are at the same VAT rate, it does not matter if you calculate your margin on a sales price including VAT, providing you do the same for all goods. If you sell at more than one rate, your margins will not be comparable unless you eliminate VAT.

To calculate the selling price net of VAT

If the net price subject to VAT at 15 per cent is 100, that including VAT is 115.

Thus, if the price including VAT is £2.50: $\frac{100}{115}$ × £2.50 = £2.17 which is the net price to the nearest penny.

Proof: £2.50 − £2.17 is 33p which is the VAT at 15 per cent on £2.17.

To calculate a selling price for an item at an given percentage margin

If you buy at 50 and you wish to earn a 30 per cent margin on your selling price net of VAT, the calculation on selling price is:

Selling price net of VAT is 100: 30% profit gives a cost of 70 so multiply your cost by $\frac{100}{70}$

Thus: $\frac{100}{70}$ × 50 = 71.43p. Proof: profit is 21.43 and $\frac{21.43}{71.43}$ = 30%.

Add VAT at 15 per cent on 71.43 = 10.71

Total 82.14 so you round down to 82p or up to 83p to give your selling price including VAT.

Alternatively, your margin of 30% = $\frac{3}{10}$. This is a mark-up of $\frac{3}{7}$. $\frac{3}{7}$ × 50 = 21.43, the same cash profit as above.

Questions involving simple business calculations
Answers below

Here are some questions to test your understanding of the various ratios previously discussed.

1. (a) What must your sales be for you to break even if your fixed costs and your gross profits are as below?

Fixed costs	*Gross profit*
(a) £100 per week	20% margin
(b) £100 per week	20% mark-up
(c) £330 per week	30% margin
(d) £330 per week	30% mark-up
(e) £330 per week	$\frac{2}{3}$ margin
(f) £330 per week	$\frac{2}{3}$ mark-up

2. Your sales are £40,000 per annum and your gross profit 25 per cent. If you cut your prices by 5 per cent how much sales must you add in order to make the same profit?

3. If you raise your prices by 5 per cent how much sales could you afford to lose before you reduce your profits?

4. Your stocks are £5,000 at cost and you turn them over 7 times. What is your cost of sales?
   Your margin is 20 per cent. What is the value of your sales?

Answers

1. (a) $100 \times \dfrac{100}{20}$ = £500 per week

   (b) $\frac{1}{5}$ mark-up = $\frac{1}{6}$ margin (16.67%)

   100×6 (or $100 \times \dfrac{100}{16.67}$) = £600 per week

   (c) $330 \times \dfrac{100}{30}$ = £1,100 per week

   (d) $\frac{3}{10}$ mark-up = $\frac{3}{13}$ margin

   $330 \times \dfrac{13}{3}$ = £1,430 per week

   (e) $330 \times \dfrac{3}{2}$ = £495

   (f) $\frac{2}{3}$ mark-up = $\frac{2}{5}$ margin

   $330 \times \dfrac{5}{2}$ = £825 per week

2. Your price cut will cost 5 per cent on £40,000 = £2,000. You must earn this by extra sales at the new gross profit, ie

   $£2,000 \times \dfrac{100}{20}$ = £10,000 extra sales needed, an increase of 25 per cent.

3. Your price increase will earn 5 per cent on £40,000 = £2,000. You can lose sales at the new gross profit thus:

   $£2,000 = \dfrac{100}{30}$ = £6,667, a decrease of 16.7 per cent.

   Alternative calculations are to apply the new gross profit margins to the gross profit sum required which gives the new sales figures.

   Thus (b) $£10,000 \times \dfrac{100}{20}$ = £50,000

   (c) $£10,000 \times \dfrac{100}{30}$ = £33,333

4. Stocks of £5,000 turned over 7 times = cost of sales £35,000. If the margin is 20 per cent ($\frac{1}{5}$) mark-up is ¼, ¼ × £35,000 = £8,750 profit. Sales are therefore £43,750.

Chapter 20

The Key Facts about Your Business Finances

The facts shown by your accounts

A variety of ratios have been mentioned in this book. These are summarised at the end of this chapter and some questions and exercises given to help you fix them in your mind.

It has been said that the key points about choosing a retail shop are site, site and site. Of running a business one could say they are gross profit, gross profit and cash, cash, cash.

Gross profit is of such significance in relation to net profit that it usually dwarfs all other profit and loss figures. Refer back to Chapter 9 if you need to revise this point.

Cash is so vital because it pays the bills. The tank chart section about cash flow in Chapter 11 emphasises this.

Ratios can tell you a great deal about the financial side of your business.

What is a key operating ratio?

Key operating ratios measure facts which matter about your daily trading, ie the activities which have a significant effect upon net profit. Examples are percentage labour efficiency and sales per square foot. Others are listed below.

Operating ratios therefore measure details on a daily or weekly basis in contrast to profit and loss or balance sheet ratios which measure overall results annually. They are vital because if daily operations are not right, the annual profit will not be either.

Which are your key operating ratios?

This depends upon your trade. Most operating ratios concern either sales, manufacturing output, gross profit or labour use since these are usually the key figures affecting profit. In retailing, for example, gross profit earned per product and per square foot of space and unit sales per product are key facts, while in a motor repair workshop it is the labour hours charged weekly to customers as a percentage of those paid to staff.

Some examples of key operating ratios

☐ Stock wastage in all its forms
☐ Labour hours sold as a percentage of labour hours paid for
☐ Overtime
☐ Sales per square foot/metre
☐ Manufacturing efficiency ie output rates per hour or per pound of wages etc, output per unit of fuel consumption or pound of capital investment etc
☐ Warehouse efficiency, ie tonnages shifted etc
☐ Vehicle running costs per mile or per ton mile or per salesman
☐ Salesman's costs per salesman or per sales call

This list cannot be comprehensive since the range of businesses is so huge. What matters depends upon your particular circumstances. With a little thought, combined with an understanding of how the main figures in your profit and loss account and balance sheet relate to each other, you should have no difficulty in identifying the ratios which matter to you.

Where do the ratios come from?

Many of the above ratios not shown on the balance sheet or profit and loss account will be available from management reports. It is important that the reporting system, which produces the figures for comparison of actual results against budget, includes such key ratios. It is often more meaningful to everybody concerned to talk in unit volumes per day or per hour than in money values.

When does value added tax affect ratios?

VAT is extracted from all figures in the profit and loss account because it is neither a cost nor an income, the net difference being paid to the government.

But VAT does appear in the balance sheet. It is part of what your debtors owe you and what you owe your creditors and is therefore included in the figures for these items. Chapter 10 illustrates the need to adjust for VAT when calculating the respective ratios for debtors and creditors.

The government may itself be a creditor or a debtor for VAT. If it is included in debtors or creditors, any such balance owing to or from the government must be extracted before calculating the ratios.

The stock valuation does not include VAT because the VAT paid has already been recovered. Its ratio is therefore not affected.

If you are using sales or purchase figures from your records rather than from your annual accounts, make sure whether or not VAT should be included and adjust as necessary.

How do I judge whether my ratios are good or bad?

There are no hard and fast rules. Businesses vary so much, even within the same trade, that what is a good figure for one may be only average for another. For example, of two concerns, one may sell largely to local authorities or other government organisations who are safe but slow payers. That company inevitably will have to give longer credit than the other. This is one of the problems of doing business with those customers, which is perhaps balanced by the advantage of steady secure orders.

Comparisons with other businesses in the same trade are usually helpful. Often the average for a given ratio, such as gross profit or stocks, is fairly well established. Before reaching conclusions based on such comparisons, consider whether all the factors involved are similar. For example, a high gross profit margin usually means efficiency, but it can also reflect high prices and poor value to the customer. In a restaurant, one can improve margins by cutting the size of the portions or the quality of the raw materials but such policies can quickly alienate the customers.

The stocks ratio can also vary considerably as a result of policy. A heavy stockholding can reflect a business built upon service; the rapid supply of technical spare parts is an example. Provided the profit margins are high enough, such a policy can be profitable.

For example, a stock of £1,000 at cost turned over three times (ie an average holding of four months) means a cost of sales of £3,000. At a gross margin of 50 per cent this means sales of £6,000 and gross profit of £3,000. If the stock turns over six times, but at a gross margin of only 25 per cent, the cost of sales will be £6,000, sales £8,000 and gross profit £2,000. To make the same gross profit of £3,000 at 25 per cent margin, sales must be £12,000 which means a cost of sales of £9,000 and a stock turn of nine.

A gross margin of 50 per cent is higher than that in many trades but the example illustrates how the arithmetic works. It is possible to make profits from stocking slow-moving goods in a wide range if the margins are big enough. Manufacturers may well make gross margins as high as 50 per cent but they will usually have heavy promotional and selling expenses which drastically cut into their margins and which make it essential to work on lower stock levels.

Interfirm comparison schemes

Many trade associations run interfirm comparison schemes and there is also the Centre for Interfirm Comparisons (8 West Stockwell Street, Colchester, Essex CO1 1HN; 0206 62274).

Such schemes provide valuable information on a range of key ratios and can show you how your business compares. In highlighting those of your figures which are above or below the average for your industry, they can help you identify and concentrate on those aspects of your business which most need attention.

Your own ratios over a period

One of the most useful comparisons can be your own ratios over a three-year period, for example, provided that the basis of the figures has remained similar and that your business has not radically altered in its nature. Such comparisons can show up trends which are free from the inevitable distortions caused by the differing nature of other businesses.

Use your common sense!

Some ratios relate directly to your own policies and business. For instance, is your debtors sales ratio in line with your policy on credit to customers? But think first. Do you have cash sales or a large chunk of business on different terms which mean that the figures need adjusting before calculating the ratio?

Are you using trade credit correctly?

If you are not taking full normal credit, you are settling your bills before you need to. Perhaps settlement discount made this worthwhile. If you obtain 2½ per cent on £100 each month if you pay in seven days, your annual cash discount adds up to £30. If normal settlement terms are one month, you are paying £100 three weeks early. This is an average of £75 tied up throughout the year on which your £30 is 40 per cent — well worth while!

If, on the other hand, you are taking more trade credit than you should, you risk straining the goodwill of your suppliers. Push them too far and they may stop all credit. Extended credit should be used in emergencies only, not as a regular practice; you are in bad trouble if something does alarm your creditors and they clamp down.

Are you earning enough to stay in business?

Your ratios may be better than the average for your industry but are they good enough? It is no good being the best in your sector if this merely means that, in a declining industry, you are losing ground more slowly than the rest.

In the long term, to stay in business, you must earn enough on the money tied up not only to pay the interest but also to finance the replacement of assets and the development of the business. If money comes from the bank, you must pay interest. If you or your shareholders provide it, you and they need an adequate return. Over and above this, however, you must invest in new equipment etc at inflated prices and you must finance growth in sales, development into new products, etc. If you do not, your business will decline. It may be slow; it may take many years, but it will happen. Low profitability means low investment, minimal maintenance of existing installations and so on.

Then one day you have to re-equip or launch a major new investment in order to compete at all. By this time overall profitability is so low that it cannot cover the interest costs of borrowing to finance the new project at inflated prices. So do not kid yourself that you can always borrow new capital. In the end, the key to survival is adequate rates of return of profit on net capital employed. Remember that, as explained in Chapter 10, my definition of this includes the bank overdraft and any long-term loans, interest being added back to the profit, since this is all the money permanently or semi-permanently in use.

Exercises on profit and loss and balance sheet ratios

Exercise 1
(Answers overleaf)
You have learnt various ratios in previous sections. Each, when applied to one figure, will produce another as illustrated in the question in Chapter 11). Use the information given below to fill in the blank spaces. Ignore VAT.

To simplify the arithmetic for you, the stocks, debtors and creditors are expressed here as ratios rather than weeks or months of throughput. Thus a stock ratio of 6 represents $\frac{52}{6} = 8\frac{2}{3}$ weeks' sales. It is often more meaningful to think in weeks which is why this method has been used in the previous chapters in preference to numerical ratios. For the purpose of this question, assume creditors relate to cost of sales.

	A	B	C	D
Sales	£8,000			
Gross profit	£2,000			£4,000
Stock ratio	6	8	4	
Mark-up %			80%	
Margin %				20%
Stocks at cost		£5,000	£2,000	£4,000
Stocks at selling		£7,500		
Debtors ratio	8	6		
Debtors value			£1,000	£2,000
Creditors ratio	3	4		5
Creditors value			£500	

Exercise 2
(Answers on page 176)

In Exercise 1 the creditors ratio was applied to cost of sales in order not to make the question too cumbersome. However, it really relates to goods purchased. Purchases vary from cost of sales according to whether stocks have increased or decreased. This exercise illustrates the point. Fill in the missing figures.

	A	B	C	D
	£	£	£	£
Opening stocks	4,000		18,000	11,000
Purchases	20,000	14,000		63,000
Closing stocks	5,000	7,000	26,000	
Cost of sales		17,000	104,000	45,000

Answers to Exercise 1

	A	B	C	D
	£	£	£	£
Sales	£8,000	£60,000	£14,400	£20,000
Gross profit	£2,000	£6,400	£4,000	
Stock ratio	6	8	4	4
Mark-up %	33⅓%	50%	80%	25%
Margin %	25%	33⅓%	44.4%	20%
Stocks at cost	£1,000	£5,000	£2,000	£4,000
Stocks at selling	£1,133	£7,500	£3,600	£5,000
Debtors ratio	8	6	14.4	10
Debtors value	£1,000	£10,000	£1,000	£2,000
Creditors ratio	3	4	16	5
Creditors value	£2,000	£10,000	£500	£3,200

Column A

Gross profit to sales = margin 25% or ¼

Therefore mark-up $\frac{1}{3}$

Cost of goods £8,000 – £2,000 = £6,000. Stockturn 6 so stocks at cost £1,000

Sales £8,000: stockturn 6: stocks at selling = $\dfrac{8,000}{6}$ = £1333

Debtors = $\dfrac{\text{Sales } 8,000}{\text{Ratio } 8}$ = £1,000

Creditors = $\dfrac{\text{Cost of goods £6,000}}{\text{Ratio } 3}$ = £2,000

Column B
Stocks at selling £7,500 × stockturn 8 = sales £60,000
Stocks at cost £5,000 so profit in stocks £2,500. Therefore mark-up 50 per cent; margin 33⅓ per cent

Margin 33⅓ per cent on sales = £20,000

$\dfrac{\text{Sales}}{\text{Debtors ratio}}$ = debtors £10,000

$\dfrac{\text{Cost of sales}}{\text{Creditors ratio}}$ (£60,000 – £20,000 = £40,000) = creditors £10,000

Column C
Mark-up $\dfrac{4}{5}$ so margin $\dfrac{4}{9}$ = 44.4 per cent

Stocks at cost £2,000 + mark-up 80 per cent = stocks at selling £3,600

Stocks at selling × stock ratio 4 = sales £14,400

Cost of sales = stocks at cost × stock ratio = £8,000

Gross profit either mark-up × cost of sales or margin × sales = £6,400

Debtors ratio = $\dfrac{\text{Sales}}{\text{Debtors value}}$ = £1,000

Creditors ratio = $\dfrac{\text{Cost of sales}}{\text{Creditors value}}$ = 16

Column D
Gross profit £4,000 at margin $\dfrac{1}{5}$ = sales £20,000

Margin $\dfrac{1}{5}$ so mark-up $\dfrac{1}{4}$ or 25 per cent

Stocks at cost £4,000 + mark-up 25 per cent = stocks at selling £5,000

$\dfrac{\text{Sales}}{\text{Stocks at selling}}$ = stock ratio 4 (or $\dfrac{\text{Cost of sales}}{\text{Stocks at cost}}$)

$\dfrac{\text{Sales}}{\text{Debtors}}$ = debtors ratio 10

Sales – gross profit = cost of sales: $\dfrac{\text{Cost of sales}}{\text{Creditors ratio}}$ = creditors £3,200

Answers to Exercise 2

A	4,000 + 20,000 − 5,000 = £19,000 cost of sales	
B	17,000 + 7,000 − 14,000 = £10,000 opening stocks	
C	104,000 + 26,000 − 18,000 = £112,000 purchases	
D	11,000 + 63,000 − 45,000 = 29,000 closing stocks	

Summary of the vital facts about your business

Key ratios shown by the profit and loss account	*Expressed in*
Gross profit	%
Wages and salaries to sales	%
Principal expenses to sales	%
Net profit to sales	%
Key ratios shown by the balance sheet	
Current assets to current liabilities	Ratio
Liquidity — the acid test	Ratio
Key ratios shown by the profit and loss account and balance sheet combined	
Debtors to sales	Days
Stocks to usage	Days
Creditors to purchases and expenses	Days
Net profit to net capital employed	%
Super profit to proprietor's interest	%

Key operating ratios
☐ See this chapter for some examples.

Questions

☐ Why does each of these ratios matter?
☐ What are the profit and loss and balance sheet ratios of your own business?
  Pause here and look at your own accounts. Fill in your own ratios in the spaces provided above. This will teach you invaluable facts about your business.
☐ What are the key operating ratios for your particular business?